Pegasus

and the Making of
Project
Independence

Pegasus

and the Making of
Project
Independence

Clyde Weatherhead

With a Foreword by Roy Mitchell

Pegasus and the Making of

Project Independence

Cover Design by the Author

ISBN: 9798647268457

To Makandal Daaga
and All the Patriots who dared and
Continue to fight for the
Establishment of the National Purpose

ACKNOWLEDGEMENTS

My most sincere thanks to Mr. Roy Mitchell, for igniting my interest and providing so much information and for preserving the original text of Project Independence. Special thanks for agreeing to contribute his foreword to this publication.

To my daughter, Ameera, for all her assistance with reviewing and proofreading the text of this book, my deepest gratitude.

Most sincerely to the People of my land who provide me with inspiration every day to speak for our future.

CONTENTS

FOREWORD

By Ernest Roy Mitchell

I am deeply honoured to have been invited to pen the foreword to this impressive body of work that Clyde Weatherhead has so patriotically undertaken. That, after almost six decades, a singular citizen would have discerned the merit in rekindling the spirit of "Pegasus" for the benefit of us all is testimony to the deep and abiding interest which Clyde has continuously displayed in championing the overall welfare and wellbeing of our beloved Nation. He must be highly commended.

The journey through the history of Independent Trinidad and Tobago has only just begun. It portends to be long and winding: meandering between awesome and, at intervals, awful.

Significant indelible milestones have already marked our footsteps along the way. The Pegasus inscription has been one such landmark.

The philosophy of Pegasus rested on the unshakeable belief that our choice of destiny is our own: the quest to liberate ourselves out of enslavement to inherited cultural divisiveness into a seamless aesthetic mosaic brought to life in the spirit of one nation, one people, one destiny: unity in diversity: planting our national emblems atop the pinnacle of that glowing but elusive hilltop from whence cometh our dream of Independence and Nationhood: aspiring and achieving together.

When we succeed, it must not be because of what we have, but how we made the most productive use of what we have; not because of what we are, but because of who, as one nation, one people, one destiny, we desire to become.

And so let it be.

For the spirit which drives our unity of purpose must never be compromised. It must continue to dwell stubbornly in our midst. This publication provides ample evidence of this endeavour.

I commend its reading for your enlightenment, the enrichment of your soul and the awakening of your spirit of nationhood convinced as I am of the endearing desire of successive generations to leave indelible marks of distinction of having passed this way.

You are invited to read, digest and enjoy. Thank you, Clyde.

Roy Mitchell
July 2020.

PREFACE

Twenty-Twenty marks 50 years of the tumultuous events of the 1970 Revolution in Trinidad and Tobago[1].

This is an important opportunity to recount and chronicle that experience for the present and future generations.

It is also an appropriate time that we should know more of the work and contributions of an organisation that was forerunner to that which emerged as the leadership of the 1970 chapter of our nation-building effort.

Coincidentally, the man recognised as the leading figure of that struggle 50 years ago was also the founder/leader of that forerunner organisation, Pegasus and its fight to infuse the spirit of Independence in the nation's early years.

Even for many participants in the events of that time the connection between Pegasus (1962-68) and the National Joint Action Committee -NJAC (1970 -) is not known.

This is because not enough is known about Pegasus, the organisation and its role in the modern history of Trinidad and Tobago.

Thirty years ago, at a symposium organised by the Institute of Social and Economic Research of the University of the West Indies, marking the 20th Anniversary of the 1970 Revolution, the recounting the story of Pegasus began.

Roy Mitchell was the storyteller on that occasion in a presentation titled **The Making of Makandal Daaga**.

I first met Roy Mitchell one evening, back in the mid-1990's in a conversation at my office as President of the Public Services Association of Trinidad and Tobago.

The Association was in the heat of a battle against the privatisation of the Water and Sewerage Authority and Roy shared some information that was indeed useful to our cause.

In 2018, while preparing for an event to mark the 48th anniversary of the 1970 Revolution, I again came across Mr. Mitchell, not in person this time, but rather via his 1990 presentation notes. Through them, I came to know of the creation and role of Pegasus, an organisation founded by Geddes Granger.

Reading his account of the history of Pegasus left me curious to understand more of how and why Granger (later Makandal Daaga) went on to become the leader of the upheaval of 1970.

Eventually, I got Roy's telephone contact and naturally it was time for another encounter with him. We sat and chatted at his home.

On one evening, three hours into our engaging conversation going back and forth from the present to the days of Pegasus or even earlier linking the figures of the tumultuous 1930's with developments in the '60s and present, we both remarked 'That is the time!'.

Our sojourn into history went on for at least another two hours.

I came to understand how and why Pegasus emerged and what propelled Granger in the direction that thrust him into the leadership of the most significant political movement since Independence - 1970.

Through this publication, that story is further elaborated and the major product of the efforts of Pegasus – its visionary Project Independence is presented in its full text and its contents explored.

Roy Mitchell's recollections of his own involvement in the saga of Pegasus were so instructive. We all owe him a debt of gratitude as a senior organiser and leader of Pegasus, for his foresight in archiving and preserving possibly the last copy of this seminal document.

His safekeeping allows an opportunity for the study of this People's Plan for nation-building for the present generation and anyone else interested in our country's development and in charting the road ahead for its future.

Clyde Weatherhead
Trincity, Trinidad
July 2020

INTRODUCTION

History, we are told, is about the past.

It is presented as History-As-Such, an ossified record of past events. More particularly, such a view of history recognises only some ordained Right to Rule assumed by those claiming to be so anointed and speaks only from their perspective.

This history is presented as being about 'good' and 'responsible' people in the leadership of sectoral, national and world affairs. It becomes the record of the acts of kings, queens, masters, captains of industry and so on and their agents – Governors, Prime Ministers, Parliamentarian, military men and the like.

The vast majority of the members of all societies, their struggles and achievements are eliminated from view and from the record.

There is another view of history though, which sees History-as-Process, as a living phenomenon.

It recognises that within social processes, there are opposing forces; those trying to maintain their Right-to-Rule on one hand and those claiming their Right-to-Be, on the other.

The existence of these opposing tendencies and forces in the co-incidence of the mardi gras (originating in the masked balls of the estate house) and of the Kamboulay (originating in the rituals and struggles of the barracks of resistance and challenge) can be seen in our country's Carnival.

It is evident in the clash between the colonial power and the masters of industry versus the colonised workers and poor in the 1937 anti-colonial uprising. .

The struggle of opposites is apparent in those who sought to preserve the colonial status quo and the persistence of the Empire against those who demanded Home Rule and Independence as expressions of the Right to Self-determination.

It is the clash of opposites and the desire to break out of the definition of History-as-Such that has exploded into open confrontation at various points in our history in various forms in our twin-island space.

In the 20th century, 1919-21, 1937, 1945-46, 1958-62, 1970-75 and other points since, have marked the intensification of that clash that has propelled the history of this land and society forward to the present.

History-as-Process allows us to understand the links; to connect the dots between the Present, the Past and the Future.

The periods of open confrontation have confirmed the desire of the vast majority of this society's members to occupy the centre stage of history and take it in a new direction, defined by them.

These moments have also shown that it is not enough to rebel against the symptoms, against society-as-such, without addressing the fundamentals of the social order – the structure that permits the rulership of the minority and the prejudices that protect it.

The appearance and work of Pegasus was an attempt to move beyond the formalities and trappings of Independence. The recognition that the country *"was not Independent in spirit"* and the desire to create *"Nationhood driven by inner spirit"* motivated its founding.

Its emergence, in the year of Independence, marked the beginning of the contest of two opposing approaches to the process of nation-building. The imposition of direction by 'anointed' practice of 'party politics' versus the participatory inclusive formulation of direction from below by an involved and empowered citizenry.

Project Independence was the Method and Plan created by the People themselves, marshalled by Pegasus, to build a society to serve their needs and the needs of all.

It was diametrically opposed to another prescription developed by those who inherited and maintained the methods of the colonial power while proclaiming 'Massah day done!'.

1970 was another step in that direction of creating Nationhood driven by inner spirit.

That desire and aspiration persists today, and its final victory awaits to be achieved in the creation of the future.

It is in this context that the birth and life of Pegasus and its special creation Project Independence are to be understood.

President General   Mr. E. Roy Marshall
Executive Director   Mr. Geddes Granger
General Secretary   Miss Barbara Bleuman

Motto
'To Educate and Elevate'

Please reply to

1 FROM HOME RULE TO INDEPENDENCE

"Without culture, and the relative freedom it implies,
Society even when perfect, is but a jungle.
This is why all authentic creation is a gift to the future."
                                        -     Albert Camus

History is a continuum.

Successive generations build on the achievements of those before them. Lessons come from those who faced the challenges of overcoming a process that threatened their very survival to begin laying the foundations of a new nation striving to inculcate a national identity while building a society.

From disparate and far-flung regions of the globe, our forebears were thrown together in this space and had the task of constructing a future together, including those they all met as its first people.

Each brought their own history, experience, language, culture, aspirations and hopes and contributed to forging the building blocks that the current generation must use to add their own in constructing the future.

The generation which straddled the colonial to post-colonial transition of the 1950's – 1960's was able to bequeath to this generation their own special creations. Pegasus and Project Independence were vital contributions they forged through the effort of many.

The Foundations

For two centuries spanning Emancipation from chattel slavery, through Indentureship, two world wars and many steps toward sovereign control of this space the trailblazers persisted.

Among the iconic moments were hoisting the banner of Home Rule in the conflagrations of the 1930's, headlined by the Butler Riots and the 1940-50's Independence movement to the achievement of Independence in 1962. Through these times, on various fronts and in various fields, the modern history of our land was forged.

At the base were the modes of production by which the natural resources were converted to products that allowed the accumulation of material wealth, mostly for the benefit of the Empire-builders headquartered in England.

The relations among the various human elements of the productive forces were formed in the process of the plantation economy.

Continuing to build our society with national spirit requires that we never lose sight of the foundations and the contributions of our predecessors; shaping our present by defining our political and social personality; by developing our scientific understanding of our physical and social space and forging our sense of self.

Economic, political, and other achievements are important. However, without the cultural capital that has been enriched over time our sense of nationhood would be desolate.

So, while the underlying conflicts, sometimes open but always present, are important to our history, the parallel endeavours in the field of culture, particularly in literature and social education must also be known and valued.

As Professor Selwyn Cudjoe noted, "*The literature of Trinidad and Tobago reflects the emergence of a national spirit that has been cradled by a specific history and culture. Studied conscientiously, it helps us to understand ourselves as a people and to promote a deeper understand-*

ing of where we have been and why we are who we are." [Selwyn Cudjoe: 2004]

We must cherish and study the literary treasures bequeathed to us by our talented and imaginative minds in all genres. They are our patrimony as much as the mineral resources beneath the surface and our productive lands.

The Crucible

Can you imagine a time where there was no priority bus route, no 4-lane highway to San Fernando, no maxi taxi, no Internet, no smart phone, almost no telephones at all.

There was such a time – A period spanning either side of World War II.

There was an atmosphere of anticipation. The prospects and the hope for change permeated the atmosphere.

Whether you were in the oilfields or the cane fields and sugar factories; whether you were in Port of Spain, on the docks or in the barrack yards or in the plantations in Tobago, everywhere a new Trinidad and Tobago was on every person's mind.

In the administrative capital, in the new industrial capital of the South, in the towns and villages across the country the conversations abounded about a new future, a future free from colonial direction from the headquarters of the Crown Colony.

With no social media, no blogs and Facebook posts, the communication was face-to-face, and the discussions were enthusiastic and animated, yet structured in the style of the debate. Debating was not reserved only for the gentlemen of the Legislative Council, nor was it the purview solely of the revered scholars and intellectuals.

Everywhere, everyone was talking about a new future – the Home Rule that Butler championed, the independent future of self-governance and determining our own destiny.

Youth groups, cultural and debating clubs, organisations of all shapes and sizes sprung up across the land, nurtured by a spirit of self-motivation among young and old alike. Everyone was eager to talk about their own future; to talk about shaping this land to which all of us, except for the remaining First Peoples, had arrived voluntarily or by force, and contributed to its economic fortune.

There was a sense of 'ours', of ownership – this land is ours. The talk was all about its future and every person's role in creating it.

Such was the crucible in which Pegasus - the organisation that was political without being partisan, was fashioned.

Its founders and leaders were direct products of the literary and debating tradition and those organisations of their time.

The Vehicles of Literacy and Literature

Emerging from the dehumanising holocaust of chattel slavery, the now-free majority of the population set about reclaiming their humanity and their right to participate in the building of this society in a land from which they could not depart.

They were eager to make their mark, not just as 'free' labourers but also in the intellectual and cultural pursuits to which the former masters claimed monopoly.

The new literary history of Trinidad and Tobago began almost immediately after the Emancipation Proclamation and the notion of Apprenticeship was not allowed to hinder its development and the entry of the new participants.

The colonial elite claimed privilege and established the Port of Spain Literary Society on September 1, 1840.

The Africans had brought with them their own imaginative though unwritten literature in the form of their folklore, the Anancy stories, riddles, and other forms of oral tradition.

When the Indians arrived with the start of Indentureship in 1845, they too brought their oral and written literature in the form of kheesas (folk tales) and religious sagas of Hosay and Ramleela and more.

The Europeans under whose control these two groups were brought together had their poetry and other forms of written literature including plays, novels, and French Creole verse.

All these linguistic sources influenced the creation of a new language which John Jacob Thomas consolidated in *The Theory and Practice of Creole Grammar.*

As Cudjoe put it "Trinidadians had developed a particular language as they located themselves in their time and place.". [Selwyn Cudjoe: 2004].

The platform for the establishment of an indigenous written literature was now establishing itself.

Jean-Baptiste Phillip's *Free Mulatto* published in 1824 is considered one of the earliest works of English-speaking Caribbean literature. [Ginette Curry: 2007].

As part of a series of slave narratives of the time, *The Interesting Narrative of Maria Jones* was produced in Trinidad in 1848.

Adolphus: A Tale written by a black Trinidadian was published in the newspaper *The Trinidadian* in 1853.

In 1854, *Emmanuel Appadocca Or, Blighted Life: A Tale of the Bou-caneers*, considered to be the first novel of Anglophone Caribbean literature, was published by Maxwell Phillip of Trinidad. [Ginette Curry: 2007].

Throughout the 1850's Maxwell Phillip and others persisted in writing and debating literary issues which led to a series of literary and historical essays by L. B. Tronchin, J. J. Thomas, Canon Philip Douglin and Stephen Nathaniel Cobham.

The indigenous tradition of writing had emerged.

The newspapers were an important vehicle and support for the emerging literature.

In its June 13, 1846 edition, the *Trinidad Spectator* published a letter that called for the creation of a "literary institution" in the country. *The Trinidadian* published several literary pieces apart from *Appadocca*.

From the earliest days of post-Emancipation life, another vehicle of literary endeavour that was to persist for more than a century was the literary and debating club. These clubs, in their structures, memberships and intensity of work varied, but they endured.

The literary and debating societies and clubs provided the platform for many of the educated as well as the uneducated to have a forum in which to express themselves and to follow the developments in the nation. These societies, along with the court rooms and the proceedings there, allowed people of different social and educational standing to be informed and educated.

With the turn of the 20th century, Stephen Nathaniel Cobham published *Rupert Gray: A Tale of Black and White*, the first novel to explore the issues of inter-racial relationships and the rising consciousness of Africans in their colonial Caribbean environment.

Joseph de Suze produced *Little Folks Trinidad* in 1901, a book that captured and catalogued the flower and fauna of our physical landscape for the first time and placed it in the hands of the children and other folk of Trinidad and Tobago.

The Literary Upsurge in the 1920's and 30's

Several coincidental developments influenced a new upsurge in the literary life of the country in the next two decades.

Some of these developments which provided momentum in both the oral and written fields of literature were:

➢ The end of Indentureship in 1917

➢ The end of the World War in 1918

> The return of Trinidadians who served in the British military with their awakening experiences and the rise of working-class consciousness influenced by the Russian Revolution

> The 1919 dockworkers and support strikes

> The strengthening of the Trinidad Workingmen's Association

> The demand by Indian and African teachers for participation in shaping education policy

> The emerging Indian nationalism alongside Garveyism

> The united presence of representatives African and Indian leaders and strengthening of working-class solidarity.

In the 20's, in pursuit of their right to participate in shaping of education policy, teachers mainly of the rural primary schools took up the mantle not pursued by their new union, the Trinidad and Tobago Teachers' Union (TTTU) formed in 1919.

The agitation was driven by emerging shapers of public opinion organised in literary and debating associations across Trinidad from Sangre Grande to Cedros and in Tunapuna, St. Joseph to Couva, Chaguanas and San Fernando.

The debate topics included: 'Should Indian Immigration be Abolished?', 'Is representative government beneficial to Trinidad?', 'Is western civilization a failure?'.

Krishna Deonarine (later Adrian Cola Rienzi), a future labour and political leader, emerged as one of the stalwarts of these debating societies.

The Garveyite Movement, the Negro Welfare Cultural and Social Association and other groups, and literary and debating clubs in Port of Spain and elsewhere also provided similar outlet for an emerging call for immediate demands and for self-government.

At the same time, the development of newspapers like the *Trinidad Guardian* and others linked to other organisations like *Argos* allied to the Trinidad Workingmen's Association and the *East Indian Weekly* continued. The latter two advanced the call for self-government and all provided outlets for local writers and literary expression.

In the 1930's two literary magazines, the *Trinidad* and *The Beacon* briefly occupied the stage. The Beacon group issued its literary manifesto and encouraged indigenous literature with *'aesthetic integrity, linguistic realism and social accuracy'*. The *Beacon* was established by Albert Gomes himself a trained journalist who went on to play a prominent political role.

The new genre called 'yard fiction' was largely based on and promoted by The Beacon's manifesto principles. This new fiction was developed by CLR James and Alfred Mendes in the mid-1920's focusing on the life, poverty and working-class culture.

Their novels, James' *Minty Alley* and Mendes' *Pitch Lake* and *Black Fauns* "were the literary offshoots of the political activities of James and Mendes in Trinidad in the 1930's.".[Leah Rosenberg: 2007]

At the same time, Seepersad Naipaul (father of VS Naipaul) was employed as a columnist with the *Trinidad Guardian.*

He was a member of the Star of India Literary Club of Tunapuna and his move to the Guardian was significant as it provided Indo-Trinidadians with a larger voice in the national press. .

His journalism provided material for his successful short story collection *Gurudeva, and Other Indian Tales* in 1943.

In this period, as Reinhard Sander put it, "the struggle for political independence and the creation of national literature went hand in hand".

That link persisted with the next wave of development of the literature in the 1950's into Independence in 1962 with writers like

Ralph de Boissiere, Samuel Selvon, V.S. Naipaul, Michael Anthony and Earl Lovelace.

Errol Hill campaigned for a national theatre and Beryl McBurnie opened the Little Carib Theatre.

The literary and debating clubs also enjoyed a revival and resurgence in this period.

As Roy Mitchell put it, *"There were literary and debating clubs. They were used by young people with ambition to debate serious issues. Youth went all over the country by bus to debates"*

"In 1962-64, they operated as debating clubs and youth movements"[2].

Among the debating clubs were Molton Hall Literary and Debating Club in Port of Spain. In San Juan/Barataria, there were clubs like Barawan, Arawaks and Saturn, led by Hugh Eastman and John Scott.

There were the San Juan Youth Movement and the Progressive Youth Movement, also in San Juan. They were let by Ramesh Deosaran and Kissoon Birsingh.

Politics was organised at the level of the youth arms of various political movements.

The Trinidad Labour Party had its youth arm and Nello Mitchell was its president for several years.

The POPPG, the Caribbean Socialist Party (CSP), and Liberal Party also had their youth arms.

New newspapers and pamphlets published by individuals like George Bowrin and Walter Annamuntudo, provide a further avenue for popular literature and expression among the population.

The 1950's also saw the emergence of public political education in the form of public lectures by Dr. Eric Williams, CLR James and others. Public debating among leading figures on national issues also commanded public attention, like the famous Eric Williams-Dom Basil Mathews debate on education.

It is out of this wave of literary endeavour in all its breadth and as its continuation, that being connected with the Literary and Cultural Club coincidentally named Beacon, established by Geddes Granger, yet another form of organisation emerged.

It was founded in 1962, the year of Independence. Its name was PEGASUS.

The mission of PEGASUS was to propel nationhood 'driven by inner spirit'.

This mission of PEGASUS is inextricably linked with the mission and value of national literature and literary endeavour as enunciated by Cudjoe's proposition that, *"The literature of Trinidad and Tobago reflects the emergence of a national spirit that has been cradled by a specific history and culture"*.

President General   Mr. E. Roy Mitchell
Executive Director   Mr. Geddes Granger
General Secretary   Miss Barbara Bowman

Please reply to

19th July, 1967.

<u>PARADE OF NATIONAL HEROES</u>

Plans are well on the way for the Celebration of this year's Independence by PEGASUS.

It is designed to pay PUBLIC TRIBUTE to our NATIONAL HEROES.

The Organisation believes that (in view of this year being the fifth anniversary), the celebrations should take a more elaborate but purposeful form, catering more than before, for a greater degree of involvement by individuals, groups or organisations representing all aspects of national life in the Country.

It was decided therefore that in addition to the usual series of Free Cultural Shows which are organised by Pegasus every year, this year's celebrations would include a Full-scale PARADE OF OUR NATIONAL HEROES through the streets of Port of Spain. Discussions are now being held with the Ministry of Home Affairs with a view to the participation of the Military Units of the Country in this exercise.

The parade is to take place on Independence Day and details of the time and route will be announced at a later date.

The Organisation has invited a number of distinguished citizens to serve on an independent panel of Judges who would select the recipients of this esteemed honour.

One of the motives behind such a project, arises out of the already well-known fact that Pegasus is not at all satisfied that the SPIRIT OF NATIONHOOD is sufficiently imbedded in the lives of our people and that very little is being done to motivate our people to develop this spirit. Pegasus fears that the Nation is bound to suffer if this absence of National Spirit is not immediately corrected.

Pegasus believes that a project of this Nature would serve in some appreciable measure to encourage this development and call on all Citizens of Trinidad and Tobago to play their part.

We feel that the exposure of our National Heroes, to the Community at large and especially to the very young or, even more, to those who for one reason or another have been forced through unfavourable circumstances not to have seen or ever heard of them before, would serve not only as an inspiration but more so as a motivating force propelling them to climb to similar or even greater heights of accomplishment through SERVICE, SACRIFICE AND DEDICATION - three very important elements of nation-building which it appears difficult to get our people to understand and appreciate.

National Heroes would be drawn from all walks of life ranging from politics to religion, economics to sports, education to arts.

Media Release issued by Pegasus Announcing
The Independence Day Parade of National Heroes

2 THE RISE OF PEGASUS

The figure of a horse has been embedded in the culture and symbolism of human civilisations. The horse has been the representation of power, strength, freedom, endurance, and elegance.

According to classical Greek mythology, Pegasus, the immortal winged horse, was born of the gods, Poseidon, and Medusa, and tamed by Bellerophon, a hero who triumphed over supernatural and earthly foes with the help of this magnificent creature.

There is also Pegasos Aithiopikos, the winged horned horse of Ethiopia, different in hue, but, representative of the same attributes as its Greek counterpart.

This legendary winged horse is also regarded as a symbol of powerful imagination and openness to new ideas.

Once formal Independence for Trinidad and Tobago was achieved, an organisation was created with the mission of answering the question of how to achieve 'true and meaningful' Independence.

It is little wonder that PEGASUS was the name chosen for that organisation.

As told by Roy Mitchell[3], *"One day after a meeting Granger told me, we all going in different directions. There is a wealth of views and perspectives, etc then nothing. It is time we lift our own thinking beyond this. We are not following up with works. Let us form an organisation doing things to benefit the whole society.".*

"Granger came up with the name".

In 1962, PEGASUS was created and built by Geddes Granger with the assistance of Barbara Blenman (Secretary at Queen's Hall), Winslow Johnson and Donald Mark.

Mitchell describes PEGASUS as *"an attempt to give direction to nation-building"* and *"an inspiration, a movement, a spirit from which great things would have been expected for Trinidad and Tobago".*

The vision was that just as the Greeks drew courage, inspiration and strength from the winged horse, Trinbagonians would also be inspired and emboldened by this broad-based organisation bearing its name.

At the same time, another force, claiming the Right to Rule and occupying positions of power vacated by the colonial operators of Crown Colony governance was pursuing its own version of the future of Independence as "responsible" government.

The contest between these two opposing tendencies persisted throughout the entire life of PEGASUS.

The Formation of the Founder

Geddes Granger was born on the 13 August 1935 on Laventille Hill, Trinidad (the house facing Quarry Street).

He was born at a time that was a very pivotal moment in the fight of the working people of this country against the colonial power for their rights and for self-determination of the nation.

His father, Gaskynd Granger, was born in Guyana and migrated to Trinidad. He was very involved in the struggles of the workers and people in the 1930s.

He was a member of the Negro Welfare Cultural and Social Association (NWCSA), one of the founders and an Executive Officer of the Public Works and Public Service Workers Trade Union in

1937, a member of the National Union of Government Employees (NUGE).

He was also active in Tobago as a member of the Tobago Peasants and Industrial Workers' Union (TPIWU) which was founded by A.P.T. 'Fargo' James[4] in 1946.

Geddes attended Belmont Intermediate School and St. Mary's College and worked at the Ministry of Finance.

Since high school, he became a powerful debater.

He, together with Roy Mitchell, Donald Mark, Otto Lennard, Winslow Johnson, Ivay Haywood, Barbara Blenman and others, went on to form the Beacons Literary and Cultural Club which used to meet at St. Ursula's School and later at the Good Samaritan Hall in Port of Spain.

Given the social atmosphere in which he was born and raised, it was inevitable that he felt the need to move beyond just debating and to build an organisation like PEGASUS.

Such were the conditions that shaped this man, who at the moment of formal Independence, took up the mission to infuse the spirit of Independence he sensed was lacking amid the spectacle of the event.

PEGASUS, for him, was to give direction to nation-building.

He created PEGASUS and later went on to become the leader of the most powerful movement of the people since the anti-colonial upheaval into which he was born in the 1930's.

Leadership Duo of PEGASUS

To undertake this vital mission, Granger mobilised the assistance of Roy Mitchell who operated as his virtual right-hand man in the years of the activities of PEGASUS.

Roy Mitchell grew up in the firmament of the anti-colonial movement with its goal of attaining Independence.

Mitchell grew up in what he describes as 'a political environment'. His father was a politician and his house on Charlotte Street in the capital was a virtual Who's Who of the likes of Tubal Uriah Butler, Albert Gomes, Dudley Mahon, Quintin O'Connor, W W Sutton, Mc Donald Stanley and many others.

Mitchell recalls Jim Barrette, leader of the Negro Welfare Cultural and Social Association, organising a discovery day ceremony and treat for the children.

His father and Gomes started the Federated Workers Trade Union. His father was also campaign manager for APT 'Fargo' James who made the first attempt at internal self-government for Tobago.

Mitchell recalls his brother, Nello, still typing the petition for James to take to London while they were driving to the airport. The petition was to be presented by APT James to Sir Arthur Creech-Jones, then Secretary of State for the Colonies.

Roy and Granger met as members of the Beacons Literary and Cultural Club.

The link between these future builders of PEGASUS was destined.

PEGASUS Takes Flight

The motto of PEGASUS was '***To Educate and Elevate***'.

Building on the tradition of the Literary and Debating Clubs and the atmosphere of public education, PEGASUS initially organised a series of panel discussions in North and South Trinidad focusing on important issues facing the country.

Panellists were drawn from the fields of trade unionism, business, education, politics, culture, and other spheres. They included: George Weekes (trade union leader), Tommy Gatcliffe (businessman), Rudranath Capildeo (politician), Melvin Robin, Andrew Carr (anthropologist), Dr. George Sammy (Engineering Lecturer/ Innovator) and Carlisle Chang (Artist).

They shared their views with the national community on a variety of topics including: 'The Education Act', 'The Closed Shop', 'T&T's Entry into the OAS', 'Apartheid' and many others.

Through these discussions, the organisation began to establish itself in the eyes of the population.

Ever mindful of the need to motivate and unify the various strands of the multi-ethnic fabric of this new nation, Granger was convinced of the value of the arts as a rallying point for moulding the unity of spirit among all citizens needed for charting its destiny.

PEGASUS took up the challenge of staging a series of concerts every night of Independence week at the Town Hall in Port of Spain.

Various art forms reflecting the cultural contributions of every colour of this rainbow nation were on show including steelband, calypso, and dance.

The artists contributed their talents free of charge – a symbolic donation to forging the identity of this fledgling nation making its way in the world.

These concerts continued for several years. As Mitchell tells, after a lengthy concert, Granger told him, "*...these people ...must have something greater to aspire towards.*". So, the idea of honouring the artists was born.

PEGASUS Awards

This idea developed into the PEGASUS Cultural Awards.

"*A PEGASUS team was established to identify various aspects of the arts and who made outstanding contributions*", Mitchell explained.

The awards were to represent both "*an expression of appreciation*" of the artists' contributions and also "*an incentive to continue the struggle with greater purpose*", continued Mitchell.

The awards were designed by the artist, Carlisle Chang, free of charge. The jewellery firm, Y De Lima made them and donated some. The rest were donated by other civic-minded businesses, as described by Mitchell.

Among the awardees were: Beryl Mc Burnie, Ellie Mannette, Sybil Atteck, Olive Walke, Vidia Naipaul, Derek Walcott, Julia Edwards, Slinger Francisco (the Mighty Sparrow), Ken Morris, Carlisle Chang, James Lee Wah (for the Secondary Schools Drama Group), Allison Alleyne and John David (for the Expo Theatre Group), Alf Codello, Earl Lovelace, Errol Hall, George Goddard, Ralph Baney, Adrian "Ball" Harper, Esmond Ramesar and C.L. R. James. Some were awarded posthumously.

The PEGASUS Cultural Awards later morphed into the National Heroes Awards.

In 1967, Granger *"felt that the people were not involved enough so that some way had to be found to give our people pride and a sense of history and achievement"*, Mitchell indicated. So, national heroes were to be honoured in addition to the artists.

The awards were presented on Independence Day. *"After the government's parade in the morning, National Heroes were named in the afternoon"*, Mitchell explained.

The PEGASUS National Heroes Awards committee developed criteria for nominations. Advertisements were placed in the newspapers inviting nominations. The advertisement read, in part: "National Heroes would be drawn from all walks of life ranging from politics to religion, economics to sports, education to arts".

Many nominations were received from several organisations and the public. The committee selected the first two awardees for their pioneering work toward the development of the county in an "unquestionable outstanding manner".

The awardees were: Arthur McShine – founder of the 'Poor man's bank', the Penny Bank which is now the National Commercial

Bank, and, Captain Arthur Cipriani – the 'Friend of the barefoot man'- leader of the Trinidad Workingman's Association and the Trinidad Labour Party.

Huge portraits of these heroes were built and on the afternoon of Independence Day, they were at the head of the heroes march, accompanied by the cadet band.

The march headed through Port of Spain; the salute was taken outside the Red House by the acting Chief Justice, Sir Clement Phillip and the march ended at the Queen's Park Savannah. The ceremonies proceeded with presentation of the awards and speeches which promoted the need for self-reliance, self-respect, and self-determination.

Activities for the Youth

By the mid-1960's, to continue the involvement of the young people and provide some focus on serious issues, PEGASUS organised National Debating Competitions throughout the country and among the secondary schools. St. Augustine High School emerged as the first winners, its successful team were Salisha Ali (later a popular tv presenter) and Gail Robinson (later an Attorney at Law, niece of A.N.R. Robinson,).

Based on a proposal from Mr. Winston Dookeran a project called the Model United Nations was organised by PEGASUS. The aim was to give the youth *"a greater appreciation of themselves as a free and independent people in the family of nations"*, as Mitchell put it.

The organising committee included: Dr. Cuthbert Joseph, Dr. Neville Linton, Dr. Yves Collart, Dr. Roy Preiswerk, Dr. Victor Isaacs, Lennox Hunte and Shastri Moonan.

As Mitchell, described, *"Students campaigned school to school for election of President of model UN. Students became Secretary General and President of the assembly. They went to do research and a key figure gave the 'State of the World' address. It was conducted like the real United Nations Assembly....*

This was never show. It was organised to enrich and develop the minds of the young people of the country. Some ended up as diplomats"[5].

Among the issues debated in the Model General Assembly were: 'The Admission of Red China to the United Nations', 'the Middle East Conflict', 'The Czechoslovak Question', 'The Universal Declaration of Human Rights', 'Conditions in Non-Independent Countries', etc.

Several prominent people came out of that activity including Anthony Gonzales, Deborah Moore-Miggins , Shastri Moonan, Victor Anthony Isaacs, Lynette Seebaran-Suite, Dave Darbreau[6], Deborah Moore-Miggins, Kenneth Valley, Harry Partap, and many others.

There was an international banquet afterwards.

The last Model UN organised by PEGASUS took place at Queen's Hall on 11 October 1967. The banquet followed at the same venue.

Building Out the Organisation

At this stage of the life of PEGASUS, Granger decided to expand the network of the organisation to various parts of the country by building branches in various communities and regions across the country.

This aspect of the organisational work was undertaken by Granger himself as leader.

Several branches of PEGASUS were established in communities including Barataria, Chaguanas, Penal, Siparia, Morvant and Port of Spain.

Through these branches many simple citizens became involved in the pioneering work of PEGASUS.

Recently, on seeing mention of PEGASUS in an op-ed by this author at least one former participant in the work of the organisation recalled his involvement in South Trinidad.

On to Project Independence

In taking the next step forward in the contribution of PEGASUS to nation-building in which all citizens were very much invested in the atmosphere of the immediate Independence period, Geddes Granger *'masterminded his most ambitious project'*, as Mitchell put it.

That was the genesis of Project Independence.,

For this most comprehensive and important project, a new level of organisation was needed to further increase the widest participation of the citizens wanting to contribute to achievement of the possibilities of Independence.

Added to the structure of PEGASUS, was a series of National Committees in which expert and ordinary citizens could make their contribution.

The Annual Convention of 1967

As part of a series of events to mark the 5th anniversary of PEGASUS in 1967, the first Convention was convened in Port of Spain on the September 22 at Kimling Restaurant.

The other events included a Meeting of all civil organisations with His Honour Mr. Cecil. A. Kelsick, Chairman of the Tax Appeal. Board as guest speaker, Model United Nations at Queen's Hall, a Young Artists Show, and an Anniversary Ball and Fashion Show at the Hilton with music by André Tanker and the Flamingos.

The anniversary events and Convention were organised by an Organizing Committee including:

Geddes Granger

Carlo Guevara

Sahadeo Maharaj

Winslow Johnson

Cipriani Lewis

Pedro Apparicio

Aldwyn Cochrane

Vaughn Thomasos

Bruce McLeod

Harvey Lewis

Lionel Roberts

Leslie Griffith

George Kingland

Winston Dookeran

Lewis Bain

Clyde Harvey

Peter Mitchell

Vernon St. Hilaire.

The Secretariat were: Barbara Blenman, Harven Lynch, and Mrs. June Cartar.

Outcomes of the Convention were the adoption of its constitution and Elected Leadership for the 1967 -71 term.

The Leadership Team elected were:

Roy Mitchell – President General

Lionel Roberts – Deputy President General

Geddes Granger – Executive Director

Carlo Guevara – Deputy Executive Director

Cuthbert Corbell – Deputy Head, External Affairs Division

Vernon St. Hilaire – Head, Finance Division

Winslow Johnson – Deputy Head, Finance Division

Dorothy Lee Yen – General Secretary

Ann Daniel – Assistant General Secretary

Malcolm Blood   Peter Mitchell – Trustees.

This anniversary celebration turned out to be the last such occasion in the life of PEGASUS.

Clipping of Newspaper Article on Pegasus
By Derek Walcott

After the winged horses, what?

THE silver-plated trophy from Pegasus, a kind of long-maned horse, prances on the bookshelf. The little horse is gallant, but it soars from a base that makes it plant. Depending on the way it is bent, it can look like one of the horses of Phaethon's chariot that fell with him when his ambition took him too near the sun, or it can assume a vertical take-off position, like a rocket.

Its most realistic angle is at, say, 25 degrees, which makes it, in racing terms, a jumper with wings. The wings, as far as I remember, do not bend.

Pegasus, not only a legendary horse, but the name of an active voluntary organisation whose energy is admirable, gives out its image every year. Nobody quite like it has existed before. Its motto "to elevate and educate", includes all of Trinidad, and, possibly mankind.

In the rain

[illegible paragraph]

[illegible paragraph]

Last year it organised huge discussions around the need for a National Arts Centre. The size and importance of its audiences were impressive, but the winged horse seemed to be plunging downward, since the discussions, which are now preserved in a report, dealt with the need rather than with the creation of such a Centre.

[illegible paragraph]

'Ole talk'

[illegible paragraph]

Because behind all such reports is the gossip that contains more truth, and the truth is that few of the individuals who swore really to the need for a National Centre would dissolve their identity in such a scheme, unless they were in charge. They have their own saddles to put on Pegasus.

Anywhere in the world there is more talk than art, but this country believes that talk itself is art, whether it is the "ole talk" of Sunday sessions or the fine talk of Committees.

The number of organisations, some of them charitable is amazing, that politely and vigorously devote themselves to doing damn near nothing, to conferences, conventions and reports, is frightening. Well, it's a young country, still fascinated by the authority of print.

[illegible paragraph]

[illegible paragraph]

There is money flowing around enough to let Pegasus do some old-fashioned drag-labour, to start building their stalls. One has to write "their", because most organisations are not really interested in centres to be shared by all the arts, but in memorials.

In the Appendix B of the report, the testimonials of individual artists vary from saintly dedication to weary cynicism.

The winged horse's head lifts and plunges, and no one wants to settle for an angle of 25 degrees. If the arts are in a sorry, ill-treated state in this country, these talkathons are not going to help. No one makes election promises about developing the popular arts. It is part of the tradition we inherited to save such things for later, and later is always when more pressing needs must be attended to.

'I pity'

The Pegasus preliminary report is one of those bills that paralyse generation, that asserts the part-fragmentary right of committees to spawn smaller committees.

And remarkable, the sort of those serious artists in this country turn their back on all the talks, and go about their work, which is a pity. But Pegasus must be commended for knowing that the day more concrete proposals are shown, they will get down and mix it themselves.

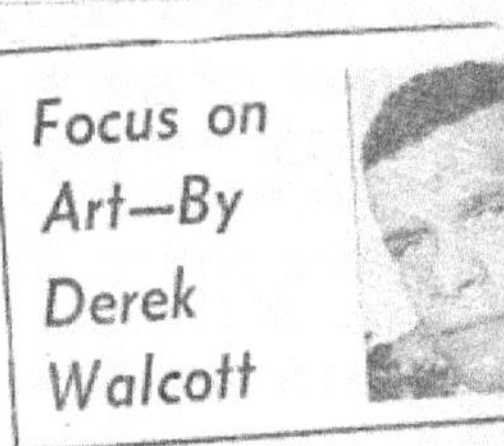

3 THE MAKING OF PROJECT INDEPENDENCE

Organisation of the Exercise

As Mitchell described it in his 1990 notes – *"Project Independence was the medium through which all the talented farces in the country were to be brought together to put in place e plan to convert the "unity of spirit" which we had been seeking to develop over the years into a new and dynamic "unity of purpose".*

This major work of Pegasus was focused on creating a plan for the all-round development of this newly independent country.

The initiative came from Granger and was decided by the National Committee of Pegasus.

Committees were established in several important project areas with participation from a wide cross-section of prominent citizens engaged in each area of activity, technical experts, and other citizens.

The Pegasus National Committees were Sports, Arts and Culture, Social and Project Port of Spain. Granger personally served on the first three of four committees.

The committees were supported by secretaries including Joan Lowhar, Annette Hart, Barbara Blenman, Marvin Lynch, Ann Awong.

The hallmark of the work of these project committees was their inclusiveness and the practice of wide participation and contribution.

Mitchell noted regarding the National Arts Centre project, *"I remember when we went to Tobago. Tobagonians were so moved (as) it was the first time …they were consulted on a national project …before a decision was taken"*.

These were volunteer committees of committed citizens working to develop plans for national development. The major work of implementation would, however, have to be undertaken by governmental agencies with the capacity to take on the actual physical work, unless Pegasus was authorised to do so.

Derek Walcott, in a newspaper article *After the winged horses, what?* lauded the efforts of Pegasus and the discussions it organised 'around the need for a National Arts Centre'. However, a bit harshly he ended with *"But Pegasus must be commended for knowing that the day more concrete proposals are sown, they will get down and mix it themselves"*.

This organisation taking the initiative to develop solutions to national development issues in today's language was a Non-governmental organisation (NGO) taking on some of what a Planning Ministry of Government would largely be responsible for.

The Pegasus committees made every effort to approach and get buy-in from Government on their various proposals.

However, as Mitchell has noted, *"Politicians assume that they exercise a monopoly on the birth of ideas or a prerogative on initiatives"*.

National Sports Committee

This Pegasus committee included several persons involved in various sport disciplines as well as sport administrators, journalists and businessmen.

The committee was chaired by Mr. Ken Gordon.

Its members included:

Vernon Charles

Gerry Gomez

George Phillips

Phil Douglin

Sir Frank Worrell

Alex Chapman

Louis Barradas

Bootins Atkins

Henry Franklyn

George Alleyne

Mc Donald Bailey

Neil Davy

Wilfred Best

Lt. Comdr. Jeoffre Serrette

Alloy Lequay

B. I. Lalsingh

Lystra Lewis.

It was to examine and make proposals on:

1. The development of sport in Trinidad and Tobago with special emphasis on national planning, organization, and general administration.

2. The erection and establishment of a National Sports Stadium.

3. The creation of an atmosphere conducive to the development of sport.

A sub-committee was asked to prepare specific proposals for the development of private playing fields for clubs and the provision of sports and recreational centres per 100,000 members of the population. Their reports were submitted to Government.

The committee commenced its work in regard of item 2 of its mandate – the National Stadium, a 30,000 seat multi-sport facility.

Meanwhile, the Trinidad City Development Company had set about the creation a new residential community between Tunapuna and Arouca in the East of Trinidad called Trincity.

The Trincity company offered to make some of its lands available for the stadium and parking facilities, as a donation to the project. Joseph Charles Bottling Works located on the Western end of the Trincity lands also offered to provide an electrical scoreboard.

Seeking official approval, but not funding, the committee took its national stadium proposal to Government. An important meeting was held with the Ministry of Education in June 1966 on details of the stadium proposal.

National Arts and Cultural Committee

This committee was set up under the chairmanship of Roy Mitchell and with participation of several persons involved in various aspects of the visual and performing arts.

The committee included:

Louis Blache-Fraser C.M.G.

Colin Laird

Carlyle Chang

David de la Rosa

Fred Thomas

Gemma Ramkeesoon, O.B.E.

Napier Pillai

Robert Montano

Esmond Ramesar.

The committee decided that a National Arts Centre was a critical asset for the development of the arts in the country. It engaged in widespread public consultation across the entire country.

The site selected was the Princess Building Grounds opposite the Queen's Park Savannah in Port of Spain. The building and grounds were already in use as a calypso venue and for other activities including sport. Pledges of financial support for the project came from various sources.

Derek Walcott's newspaper article, already referred to, verifies the work of the committee.

Subsequently, the committee took its next step – taking the proposal to Government.

National Social Committee

The Social Committee was chaired by Senator Rev. Roy Neehall.

Included among its members were many people involved in different aspects of social work and social development including religious leaders of various persuasions.

The members included:

Mr. Ken Hill

Mrs. Cleopatra Barnes

Dr. E.L.S. Robertson

Asst. Comm. Cyril Barnes

Professor Egbert Tai

Mr. Albert Pereira

Dr. Wahid Ali

Mrs. Ahilyn Mohan

Mr. George Goddard

Fr, J. Lai Fook

Dr. James Millette

Rev. J. Sewell

Mr. De Wilton Rogers

Pandit Karoo Omah Maraj

Mr. W.W. Sutton

Rev. Idris Hamid

Mr. George Collymore.

The committee viewed the social development of a nation as "the process of growing and maturing for all individuals as citizens of a single nation in all their relationships with each other, with their physical and material environment, with existing institutions and with the world at large".

It outlined its work as to:

> conduct research in the many areas of social development.

> study related problems and issues.

> make known their findings far the benefit of all but especially for those who may be planning specific projects.

> assist in securing greater coordination of effort among all existing agencies engaged in social development.

The committee recognised the many agencies, societies, organisations both governmental and non-governmental and the need to avoid those in need from slipping through the cracks by developing 'total coordination' among those bodies.

Project Port of Spain Committee

"Project Port of Spain" was conceived as a project designed to redesign and reconstruct the City of Port of Spain along modern metropolitan lines to solve the problems of a "rapidly expanding city, spreading without a semblance of order' consuming the suburbs without regard for beauty, safety or economy".

The committee was chaired by Mr. Louis Blache Fraser, C. M. G.

Members were:

Dennis Mahabir

Colin Laird

Roy Mitchell

Napier Filial.

Many professional experts offered their services on a voluntary basis and the Prime Minister even agreed to professional Civil Servants assisting in their private capacity. The Trinidad Chamber of Commerce offered to have three of its members work with the committee.

International agencies were approached and showed interest in the project.

The committee was of the view that the business community would assist when funding was needed for detailed planning work to be done later.

Producing the Blueprint

The development of Project Independence was conceived as addressing the four most critical areas of national life – political, social, cultural, and economic.

According to Mitchell, *"The group met for months, day and night, putting the act together, delegating, planning and launching"* this most ambitious of all Pegasus projects.

The National Committees in various subject matter areas worked through most of 1966 to produce this *'comprehensively spelt out national plan'*, as Mitchell described the Project Independence document.

This was an enormous planning exercise taken on as an initiative of the people, many contributing their time, skills, and talents and developed through the broadest consultation within Pegasus and among the population.

This was the People's effort to chart the development of the nation on a non-partisan basis and to look after their own welfare.

The document itself invited further input from anyone who would read it and had any suggestions or criticisms to offer.

When the document was completed, a date was set for its public launch in Port of Spain. The venue was decided as the Public Library on Knox Street.

The President of the Senate, Mr. J. Hamilton-Maurice agreed to be the feature speaker.

The Pegasus members were anxious for this important event.

The venue was booked. The time was set at 6:00 p.m.

A newspaper mobilisation campaign was implemented to invite the public.

The Last Straw – Sabotage of the Launch

Throughout the work of Pegasus, at every stage from its initial debate events to its Cultural and later National Heroes awards to the undertaking of Project Independence, Pegasus established itself as a serious influence and leading force among the people.

The activities were timed around Independence Day and focused on the path to the development of the independent nation.

Those who were championing the road of party politics and claimed a right-to-rule became increasingly concerned at these initiatives of the People for which officialdom could claim no credit.

The political directorate were becoming overly concerned about being upstaged and reacted.

When the National Heroes Awards march and ceremony was held, the reaction from the political hierarchy was of intimidation including *'sending spies to monitor our movements'* and *'some police harassment at our homes'*, as Mitchell described it.

Mitchell tells the story of the idea of these awards this way, "*My experience in India - I went to a conference and sat where the Prime Minister, etc sat and there was a parade. It was something to behold. Every province marched and put on displays based on what was indigenous to their area.*

We tried to get government here to do something like that so the communities could prepare and organise something".

The Pegasus awards at Independence had pre-dated the official national awards ceremony.

With every proposal coming out of the National Committees established by Pegasus as part of the Project Independence process, when presented to Government, were either ignored or an attempt to was made to absorb and stifle the initiative or presented as if they were a Government initiative..

For example, the National Stadium project proposal was taken to the Education Ministry in June 1966.

Instead of the promised studies being undertaken, on September 24 Government announced the appointment of its own official national stadium committee on which several members of the Pegasus committed were included.

The proposed location close to the airport, with land donated by the Trincity Development Committee, etc were all abandoned.

A national stadium was only opened by Government in Port of Spain 18 years later.

Despite several meetings with Government and requests for the release of the Princess Building Grounds site to Pegasus as the location for the National Arts Centre, nothing happened.

One committee after another was set up by Government with no action.

In 2009, 43 years later, the National Academy of the Performing Arts was opened on the same location that the Pegasus Arts and Culture committee proposed for the National Arts Centre.

Proposals from the National Social Committee met with a similar fate with inaction by Government.

So, too, the plans for the re-development of the capital city out of Project Port of Spain were scuttled and many administrations and promises later, yet another Government redevelopment plan was on the drawing board 54 years later.

The last straw came on the afternoon when Project Independence was to be launched at 6:00 p.m. by the Senate President at the Public Library on Knox Street in the capital.

As Mitchell tells it, "*At around 2:00 to 3:00 p.m., loudspeakers were going through the streets of Port of Spain announcing a PNM meeting at Woodford Square for the same time*".

The ruling party hastily called a public meeting just opposite the venue of the Pegasus launch. The sabotage was evident.

Commenting on this incident, Mitchel said, "*Admittedly one of the intimidating features of 'Project Independence' was the fact that the study document took on the face of an election manifesto and would therefore have understandably caused microscopic lenses to be placed on any organisation which produced such a document .... We obviously loomed high as a political threat*".

He went to describe what he saw as the attitude of the ruling party and its leader to initiatives of a non-party organisation in matters of governance and nation-building this way, "*No person or organisation contributed in the past, contributes now or will contrib-*

ute in the future, to the development of Trinidad and Tobago but the PNM all things begin and end in the heart of the PNM[7]".

Over the next few months, a deliberate campaign to destabilise Pegasus was launched. "*Williams got PNM people inside Pegasus to try and sabotage it*", Mitchell said.

Efforts were made to foment distrust between the principal leaders and encourage factionalism within the organisation.

The constant sabotage of the efforts of Pegasus as a non-governmental organisation by the 'responsible' government exerted tremendous negative pressure on Granger and the organisation.

As Mitchell records in his 1990 notes, "*More frustration for us, greater frustration for Granger. The result – more determination (by Granger) to bring Williams to his knees*".

The government's opposition to the nation-building efforts of Pegasus only served to 'radicalise' Geddes Granger.

Eventually, after the 1967 National Convention, Granger moved on to the next phase of his fight for "'*nationhood with inner spirit*" by building "*organisation doing things to benefit the whole society*".

He took his fight for the country's independent development to the University of the West Indies when he enrolled as a student in 1968 and went on to become the President of the Students Guild.

He was on a trajectory which led him to the creation of the National Joint Action Committee and leadership of the 1970 Revolution, called the Black Power Revolution, the most significant mass political movement in the country's history since the tumultuous 1937 Butler Riots.

At the heart of these developments, is the fundamental contradiction between the political parties and the People as the party claims complete dominion over matters of national affairs and deprive the People of their role in such matters or attempt to do so.

Who sets the agenda for the society's development? That is the question.

4 A PEOPLE'S PLAN FOR NATION-BUILDING

Project Independence, the plan, was the product of the experiences, expertise, ideas and proposals of many.

As Roy Mitchell put it, "*'Project Independence' was the medium through which all the talented forces in the country were to be brought together to put in place a plan to convert the "unity of spirit" which we had been seeking to develop over the years into a new and dynamic "unity of purpose".*

"The Group met for months, day and night, putting their act together, delegating, planning and launching".

This was an effort, conducted with the widest possible inclusion of the People of Trinidad and Tobago to develop their own plan and programme for the building of the nation in the spirit of the initiatives of Independence, unfettered by partisan politics and governmental officialdom

It was the first attempt by citizens to define for themselves the road to the future for the society with their own vision and in their own interest.

Project Independence lays down principles, presents a vision, encourages participation in decision-making, heralds institutional developments, anticipates difficulties, proposes solutions and reminds citizens of their role and duties as builders of the society.

The efforts of all those patriots who helped craft this People's Blueprint five years after Independence demands a serious examination of its contents.

THE PREAMBLE

> "The goals we propose are not beyond us. We have the human and material resources. But first there must be a deeper understanding by the entire population of the present state of the nation., and a greater interest in its possible future course. No less essential is the inculcation of a sense of urgency, of duty, of service and of sacrifice."

From the outset this roadmap for nation-building focuses on the link between the individual, the collective and the society as a whole. It stresses the role, duty and social responsibility of the individual for the entire success of Independence and nation-building project.

It expresses a profound confidence in the capability of the People as the beneficiaries and guarantors of Independence to solve the problems and staunchly build the nation.

It advocates the values of duty, service and sacrifice for the common good.

It recognises the important role of the individual in the achievement of success for all.

> "The welfare of all must never be sacrificed on the altar of individualism and sectionalism. But this is bound to continue as a national problem if the absence of National Purpose in the life of the nation is not immediately corrected. National purpose must precede and influence sectional interests and this alone will lead to resolute endeavour on the part of all individuals and groups to work

for the general welfare, development and happiness of
the whole nation of Trinidad and Tobago."

Project Independence emphasises the importance of the social
agenda of nation-building and decries the promotion of individual or sectional (sectarian) interests over the social interests of
the nation as a whole.

It emphasises the critical role of defining and the effort at achieving the National Purpose decided by consensus among those who
constitute the nation and not the paramountcy of special interests.

> "Indispensable to the fulfilment of National Purpose is
> careful planning. A charted course, with the route sign-
> posted by well-defined gaols and objectives is essential."

Project Independence was not just a visionary document, it was a
project plan for the nation-building project guided by the vision
set by the National Purpose.

Planning with defined goals and objectives necessary for continuous assessment and adjustment where required were embedded in the project planning approach espoused by Pegasus in the
firmament of the early Independence years.

> "However, no plan, though well-conceived, no goal,
> though clearly stated, can be successfully achieved un-
> less those who stand to benefit are involved in and identi-
> fied with the project from the very inception."

Consistent with Pegasus' method of work and encouragement of
participation in the work of nation-building, the critical role of
free and conscious participation of the People in decision-making is clearly articulated.

> "All are important and everyone is invited to share our
> ideas and to add their own and then together to work to-
> ward their implementation and fulfilment."

Even after the development of the first draft of this nation-building Plan, those for whom it was developed are encouraged to further subject it to their own analysis and examination and contribute their ideas to improve it further.

Most importantly, they are then called upon to work for its successful implementation in their own and the interest of the nation.

This was the embodiment of the entire raison d'etre and spirit of Pegasus focused on nation-building by cementing the unity of spirit of Independence founded on the People's participation in decision-making about the future.

SPECIFIC PROGRAMMES

Beyond the general vision and statement of principles, the nation-building plan goes on to present a series of specific programmatic proposals representing the "sign-posts", "goals and objectives" the importance of which was recognised in the preamble.

Project Independence was at once a statement of aspiration and a practical plan for achieving the National Purpose.

Mitchell speaking of the details of Project Independence, said: "*In it, we identified the four most critical areas of national life, the political, the social, cultural and economic.*".

In the areas specified under each heading the text starts with a statement of principles on the particular subject area.

<u>POLITICS</u>

> "We believe that the chief political aims of the nation should be the general development, welfare and happiness of all peoples therein and that the political framework should be adapted to the special characteristics of the people at any period of their development and that

the experiences of others who have achieved or are achieving nationhood be considered in framing the laws of the body politic.".

For Pegasus, the purpose of politics is the satisfaction of the needs and guaranteeing the rights of all within the society.

As a matter of principle and policy, the political framework should develop as the people and relations within the society develop. Politics must move with the times and serve the requirements of the stage of development of the society.

The political framework (governance arrangements) must be based on the experience of the people of this nation and that of others elsewhere in their own nation-building projects, with the full participation of all citizens engaged in decision-making.

This is a far cry from the notion of politics as a matter of a dominant party domain serving what the document calls "sectional interests".

This view of politics is consistent with the overall principle of the pursuit of the "National Purpose" being the driving force of Independence and nation-building.

Politics according to Pegasus was what Lloyd Best later called Politics with a big "P", that is, understanding the relations among the social forces in the society and acting always toward achieving the National Purpose. This was the opposite of the politics with a small 'p', the perpetual partisan contest aimed at attaining or continuing officeholding and non-productive adversarial posturing.

With this guiding outlook, specific programme items are proposed to achieve the kind of electoral and political processes and practice envisioned.

Project Independence addressed the issues of the responsibilities of political parties and individual politicians as well as of each citizen and his/her political duties and responsibilities.

On the role of the parties, the values they should adhere to and their duty to defend the unity of the People it proposed:

> "...that political parties make as a principal objective the attainment of harmony in the Society, especially amongst the ethnic groups;

> that to this end, such parties must base their appeal on principles and ideals, on organisation and discipline and on the quality of their members"

Project Independence spoke to the issue of integrity of politicians including personal financial accountability and proposed what was the forerunner to the Integrity in Public Life Act which was enacted some twenty-three years later.

> "...lest confidence in political authority be undermined there be close scrutiny of candidates elected to office, and that records of their liabilities and assets and sources of investment be made public"

On the relationship between elected and electors and the duty of elected representatives to champion the views and interests of the electors and be accountable to them, as stewards of their constituents or burgesses, it projected:

> "...candidates of the parties elected to office should at specified periods consult with their electorate and be disposed towards being consulted at fixed times to hear legitimate grievances and complaints and to learn of the needs of the people"

and

> "...on matters of grave national concern there should be maximum consultation with the people prior to decisions being taken"

This latter issue seems to have anticipated the demand for the inclusion of referenda provisions in the country's Constitution which has gained much public support particularly in the current millennium.

It also spoke to the role of the elected Opposition as a Parliamentary force to ensure Government accountability and make its own contribution to Parliamentary decision-making on behalf of the citizens, with responsibility.

Project Independence called not for opposition for the sake of opposition, but for developing a serious alternative point of view and governance plan. It put it this way:

> "...such parties as may form the opposition should at all times offer constructive criticism of government decisions and should endeavour to be prepared to form the alternative government;"

Project Independence advocated a participatory approach to politics and governance. It took the view that politics (the relations among social forces in society) is not the domain of a special select group of citizens perceived as having special capability in the sphere of society's affairs.

It spoke to the political responsibilities of citizens and civil society organisations and the need for their attention to and involvement in political affairs and the achievement of the National Purpose.

Project Independence said:

> "the general public be no less aware of matters of political importance;

> "awareness of and involvement in political matters is tantamount to a moral responsibility of every citizen who should seek to learn of the affairs of the Country and to express fearlessly but reasonably his views on public matters:"

Political responsibility was seen as a duty, a social responsibility to be educated in and express political views for the benefit of society and participate in decision-making for its development.

> "voluntary groups and other organisations play a more

> vibrant role in forming, developing and making articu-
> late public opinion;

> "no citizen of Trinidad and Tobago regard himself as an
> intransit resident bound for an ancestral land, but as one
> permanently involved in and capable of contributing to-
> wards the national welfare;".

In this way, each citizen would be invested in the future of the society in a manner which was beneficial to all and not to narrow interests.

Nor did the role of the media in nation-building and achievement of the National Purpose escape its attention.

> "...the role of the Press as an independent and impartial
> organ of public opinion be emphasised;".

The regular evaluation of the effectiveness of the organs of governance and the service delivery was envisaged as a continuing responsibility of the nation-building project.

With a focus on the need for constantly improving the structure and functioning of the organs of governance and the "necessity for adjustment" as part of society's development, recognised in the preamble, Project Independence recommends:

> "...a reassessment of our institutional framework with
> special regard to.... the functions of political institu-
> tions"

Fully appreciating the need for direct governance at the ground level, and as if in anticipation of the current demands for more effective local government structures and community govern-ance, it proposes:

> "...reappraisal and definition of the functions of local
> councils to ensure effective areas of operation.".

ECONOMICS:-

> "We believe that our economic organisation should allow for the maximum utilisation of our human and material resources and should be capable of promoting the general welfare of the citizens and at the same time maintain the dignity of man.".

Consistent with the principles articulated in the preamble, Project Independence argues that the purpose of economic development focuses on the efficient organisation of human and natural resources for fulfilling the needs of the People.

This statement of vision emphasises that economic relations must uphold the dignity of man. This vision is also consistent with the statements of principle in the preamble of the Constitution of Trinidad and Tobago, possibly more clearly expressed.

Unlike the official economic policy in existence even before Independence - Industrialisation by Invitation - focused on 'screwdriver' industries funded by external investors, Project Independence in its Economic policy and programme pays attention to multiple sectors including Research and Development, Industry, Agriculture, Project Efficiency, People's Participation, Savings and Reinvestment, Co-operatives, Buy Local, Regional and International Trade.

Thus, a wide spectrum of economic matters and labour relations and labour market issues are also addressed.

All of these factors linked to the overall vision of the economy '*promoting the general welfare of the citizens*'.

Project Independence also spoke to the importance of promoting economic activity among the communities and developing a culture of saving and investment, as opposed to consumerism by individuals and communities alike.

> "...education of the community on the economics of everyday life be given so as to effect greater participation by the community in the economic activities of the Nation

> "...such participation reveal itself in greater efforts to save money and that moneys saved be invested in local enterprise"

As part of the notion of Independence, the promotion of buying local was an element of the economic thinking behind Project Independence. The development of the national economy and reducing dependence on imported products was to be fostered.

Along with the push for investments within communities, Project Independence promoted the development of the Co-operative movement and sector as a valuable part of the comprehensive economic development of the society.

> "...efforts be made to break down the resistance to and the lack of appreciation for local produce

> "...educate the community more thoroughly on such efforts, and to adopt those features of Co-operatives as are applicable to our society".

Understanding the importance of developing a diverse and balanced economic base, emphasis was placed on the promotion of agriculture in a manner which was completely different from the old image of back-breaking plantation labour of the pre-Independence era.

The encouragement of participation in agriculture was to be promoted at every level of education together with the promotion of modern agricultural production utlising modern and constantly improving technology and efficient Land Use:

> "...reappraisal of the role of the farmer in the economy... offering inducements to our young men and women towards making agriculture a career

> "…fullest possible use be made of the Faculty of Agriculture of the University of the West Indie, and other established agricultural institutions, facilitating the agricultural development".

Paying attention to the importance of regional and international links, Project Independence call for focus trade and other relations within the region and globally.

The notion of 'forming a Caribbean Economic Association' was the harbinger for what was later to become CARICOM.

The important role of this small but Independent nation as a member of the global family of nations was also recognized and promoted.

> "..need to focus our attention abroad … within the Caribbean with a view to forming a Caribbean Economic Association, and outside of the Caribbean – to seek markets for our produce and to maintain proper and effective international relations with other countries with the aim of fostering the economic growth of our Country.".

EDUCATION:-

> "We believe that true Education is the development of the entire personality of the individual – his physical, intellectual and spiritual faculties, and that our educational system should be so structured as to allow such development.".

The entire work of Pegasus was geared to the broad education of the body politic to encourage all to make their contribution to building the nation and fostering the spirit of Independence and the all-round development of the individual.

The organisation also engaged the students and youth in a broader experience of education through debates and the model

United Nations which it pioneered.

In its every activity, it engaged in research into the various areas of social life and developed policies and programmes for the improvement of the several sectors.

It is easy to see from that experience that in Project Independence the proposals focus on stressing the value of education, encouragement of intellectual curiosity, research and formal and informal life-long learning.

It stresses the use of indigenous materials and making education relevant to the society's needs.

Project Independence promoted the notion of Education as a process of life-long learning, not merely as a matter of certification.

Education in this blueprint is about the all-round preparation of each new generation as future citizens contributing to the nation-building project.

> "education be considered not merely in terms of acquisition of knowledge but the proper use of such knowledge and not only as a period of time devoted to learning in school, but a continuous process throughout life

> "students be encouraged to develop intellectual curiosity and enquiry and to examine and analyse ideas and opinions, and consequent upon this that discussion groups and debating societies be established at all schools

> "the educational system must place emphasis on moral values and the development of creative ability".

The use of the means of mass communication as a tool in the process of education was also envisaged. This was a visionary concept at a time ahead of the explosion of the phenomenon of the mass media and later social media revolution.

This, along with a focus on education of the working age and older generation, as part of life-long learning was anticipated.

"fuller use be made of radio, television and press as media of education, and that greater attention be given to the organisation and extension of the library services

"a comprehensive plan for adult education be instituted".

Project Independence promoted the role of education as preparation for economic contribution as well as impacting social and cultural issues focusing on the needs of the present for advancing economic development and an understanding of history.

Fulfilling these important mandates, the document recognised, requires continuous innovation in what is taught as well as how to meet the evolving needs of development. .

"enquiry and analysis as may be conducted in various fields embrace the social issues of the day

"the school curriculum be so adjusted as to meet the demands of our rapidly changing society

"greater emphasis be placed on technical and scientific training, especially with regard to our industrial and agricultural development

"the history of the West Indies, particularly the history of Trinidad and Tobago, be made a compulsory study in all schools".

THE ARTS:-

"Cultivation of the Arts adds enrichment to life and serves as a unifying force in our community.".

Pegasus, in celebration of Independence and in the hope of fostering the spirit of Independence and creating the spirit of unity among the People, focused on the arts and artistic talents of the various ethnic strands of the tapestry of the population as its vehicle.

It moved from organising free concerts in celebration of Independence to honouring and showing appreciation for the contributions of the artists to nation-building through the Pegasus Cultural Awards.

It developed a plan for the establishment of a National Arts Centre which was conceived as a living cultural arts village.

Project Independence presses the arts and culture into the service of the nation-building project and also envisages mechanisms to recognise, reward and appreciate the nation's artists.

The contribution of the arts to the building of the character of the Independent citizen of the future and in the building of relations with others was recognised.

Project Independence envisaged the arts as a nation-building tool and promoting unity and harmony within the diversity that is the demographic structure of the social fabric of the nation.

> "efforts be made to develop a consciousness of, and appreciation for our cultural heritage

> "in Trinidad and Tobago, the community should show mutual respect and appreciation for our varied cultural forms

> "cultural exchanges, especially within the Caribbean, should be encouraged".

Attention was also focused on both protecting the well-being of the artists encouraged to make their contribution to achievement of the National Purpose and using the arts and culture for building relationships among the Caribbean family and further afar.

> "provision should be made to ensure that the artists' rights and rewards are guaranteed.".

> "cultural exchanges, especially within the Caribbean, should be encouraged".

The importance of institutional development for the promotion and safeguarding the cultural heritage as a platform for the future was obviously recognised and promoted.

This was a building upon the work undertaken previously by Pegasus in its early efforts to rely on the artists in invigorating the spirit of the nation and its proposals for a National Arts Centre and other such institutions.

> "facilities should be made available for students of cultural research, and measures be adopted to preserve our native art

> "established a centre of Industrial Arts and Designs, an Arts Centre and small theatres which will give institutional focus and direction to the place of the Arts in the community".

The preservation of the contributions of generations past to the cultural treasury and the promotion of those contributions to the forging of the rich cultural tapestry of this emerging nation were emphasised.

> "a group specialised in the field be delegated to chronicle our culture, seeking out the older folks, the peasants and communities that have retained much of the original Afro-Asian influences, and that books related to same be written and placed in our libraries and schools".

<u>CARNIVAL</u>:-

> "Carnival has become an intrinsic feature of the life and expression of the people of Trinidad and Tobago. As a consequence, we advocate that there should be an appraisal of this national festival…".

One of the earliest activities organised by Pegasus involved the steelband, calypso and other art forms in a series of public concerts in the week of Independence to celebrate nationhood and help artists gain respect, recognition and appreciation.

It is out of that focus on the arts that Project Independence approaches the Trinidad Carnival and proposes an all-sided approach to this 'intrinsic feature of the life and expression of the People of this nation'.

Project Independence recognizes the need to preserve the special and historical attributes of this indigenous festival and safeguard it from the pressures that seek to convert it into a mere 'valve for letting off steam' of the pressures of life and its stresses or a perpetual party or 'experience' of debauchery for the pleasure of others.

It also recognizes its potential contribution to the economic and overall development of the society of this special contribution of this nation to the treasury of world culture.

It encourages understanding of the "aesthetic, moral and social value" of this special creation and contribution of this nation to world culture and its "psychological and emotional importance to the people".

It calls for "appraisal of this national festival" from the angles of:

> "its organisation and management

> "the development of the artistry and craftsmanship

> "its economic value to the community

> "benefits and rewards derived by those who participate in the Festival, and

> "its tourist potential."

<u>SPORT</u>:-

> "Physical well-being of a nation is reflected in the number and variety of its citizens who are engaged in organ-

ised sports…".

Pegasus had long understood the value of sport for the all-round development of the individual and for the society as a whole.

Its Sports Committee had proposed the development of sporting facilities within the communities, for clubs along with the construction of a national stadium to promote the development of higher levels of sporting activity.

This was consistent with its appreciation of the value of sport on a mass level as well as for the talented athletes and sports men and women who would represent and bring glory to the nation.

Project Independence followed and expanded on those directions pointing to the importance of sport to social development, the need to improve organisation of sporting disciplines, associations and facilities.

The role and value to the well-being of the individual and community is emphasised among the proposals which include:

> "greater interest and participation in organised games and sports would serve as a curb on anti-social behaviour and afford more wholesome use of leisure

> "in a multi-racial society such as Trinidad and Tobago the integrative value of organised games should be recognised".

In the sphere of the competitive aspect of sport and the development of the talented and gifted sportsmen and women as representatives of the nation, the importance of the development of well-organised sport administrations was fully understood and promoted.

The idea of developing such organisations without reliance on the coffers of the state maintaining their financial and managerial independence was also treated as the approach to be adopted in building such important administrations.

> "the present structure of sporting bodies and clubs should be reorganised in order to encourage and facilitate the fullest development of the athletic talents of the nation;
>
> "better organisation and planning are required of sporting bodies in the selection and preparation of teams for national and international competitions;
>
> "greater resourcefulness and self-reliance be shown in the implementation of their programmes such as fund-raising projects, etc.".

Project Independence also pointed to the need for the all-round improvement of sporting facilities to encourage participation at both competitive and community levels.

> "the general improvement of sport in the territory demands adequate provision of grounds, facilities, and training, and in this connection sporting bodies and clubs should exercise greater initiative in the acquisition of same.".

RELIGIOUS, MORAL AND SOCIAL:-

> "Our pattern of social behaviour should permit and encourage freedom of religious teachings and practices, the development of moral ideals and principles, and should enable its members to live in harmony and mutual respect.".

As Roy Mitchell made plain to this author during our conversations, Pegasus was about Nationhood driven by the inner spirit *"towards the ideal you wish to become"*.

Out of that concern for nation-building and the youth, in particular, it was inevitable that its nation-building Platform would focus attention on the building and maintenance of healthy social relations among the People.

Independence, after all, is founded on the need to eliminate the old prejudices fostered by an oppressive and divisive past.

Central to this was the idea of building unity based on mutual understanding and respect.

As if anticipating the level of social and spiritual decay into which the nation has fallen as it approaches the end of the 6th decade of Independence, Project Independence offered several prescriptions and pointed to the roles of various groups within the social structure.

To the citizens generally, the drive for fulfilling the National Purpose is to be encouraged by:

> "our social life should reflect the cosmopolitan nature of our society, our adherence to the concepts of the brotherhood of man, the dignity of the individual and fundamental spiritual values of love and charity

To the religious bodies, pursuit of the goals of building the nation:

> "...social justice should be of the primary concerns of religious denominations

> "greater co-operation amongst the religious bodies to come to terms with the social issues of the day

As an important factor in nurturing health of the social environment, strengthening of the family, women and youth and preparation of the next generation to continue the task of nation-building were understood and promoted as vital for further rise of the nation:

> "family life be encouraged and ... people be made more aware of responsibilities, values and sanctity of marriage

> "our womenfolk regard themselves as "architects of our new nation" and endeavour to assert themselves as a moral and inspirational force in the community;

> "a reorientation of the attitude and outlook of our
> youths, and in this respect, there should be a reappraisal
> of the role and functions of the youth organisations in
> the community"

Strengthening the institutions for social development to supplement the efforts of the citizens in their family and other societal units was also envisaged:

> "...the establishment of Social Research Institutions to
> assist the society in awakening national consciousness
>
> "a more systematic and scientific approach to the socio-
> logical problems of the day, emphasising the need for the
> necessary social skills for those engaged in social work".

The value of assisting the vulnerable and those who may fall victim to behaviours that violate acceptable social norms, what has come to be recognised as part of the social safety net and caring for those negatively impacted by anti-social behaviour was also recognised:

> "means be provided for the rehabilitation and welfare of
> victims of violence and assault".

Apart from improving the social environment, Project Independence also projected the need for attention to the physical and natural environment and public property long before preservation of the environment became a global concern:

> "the community should show some interest in the beau-
> tification, of its surroundings, the maintenance and care
> of public parks and beaches, and the landscaping of our
> roads and highways".

First Page of the Project independence Document

<u>P E G A S U S</u>

"PROJECT INDEPENDENCE"

"Project Independence" was conceived by the National Committee of
Pegasus , which comprises representatives of our branches in Barataria,
Chaguanas, Penal, Siparia, Morvant and Port-of-Spain. We have attempted
to project our vision beyond the immediate demands of our members to the
national horizon in order to satisfy the needs of the whole community. In
this project we reflect our deep concern about the major aspects of our
national life.

The goals we propose are not beyond us. We have the human and material resources. But first there must be a deeper understanding by the entire population of the present state of the nation, and a greater interest
in its possible future course. No less essential is the inculcation of a
sense of urgency, of duty, of service and of sacrifice. The welfare of all
must never be sacrificed on the alter of individualism and sectionalism.
But this is bound to continue as a national problem if the absence of
National Purpose in the life of the nation is not immediately corrected.
National purpose must precede and influence sectional interests and this
alone will lead to resolute endeavour on the part of all individuals and
groups to work for the general welfare, development and happiness of the
whole nation of Trinidad and Tobago.

Indispensable to the fulfilment of National Purpose is careful planning.
A charted course, with the route sign-posted by well-defined goals and objectives is essential. This does not preclude the necessity for adjustment
to meet the challenge of rapid and bewildering social changes that are
commonplace in the present modern age. The machinery of society must be
geared to perform with maximum efficiency onward the attainment of these
goals. However, no plan, though well conceived, no goal, though clearly
stated, can be successfully achieved unless those who stand to benefit are
involved in and identified with the project from its very inception.

For this reason we organise public lectures to give opportunity to
those trained and experienced in various disciplines to express their views
on questions of national concern. Besides, we have promoted other activities
such as sports contests in celebration of discovery and Independence of
Trinidad and Tobago, thereby endeavouring to impress upon the minds of our
citizens [illegible] methods, and in popularising the
cultural [illegible] of our needs. In addition, we [illegible] cultural [illegible]
to people [illegible], as well as to participate in the develop-
ment of the area, endeavouring to [illegible] with its proper relation to the important role which Pegasus plays in the building of our nation.

With the purpose thus included in this endeavour to cover aspects of
our national life, we [illegible] recreation, religion, education, sports, [illegible]
[illegible] agriculture. Our goals have never have been more liberal than [illegible]

5 PROJECT INDEPENDENCE –

THE DOCUMENT

The full text of the Project Independence document introduced by Pegasus in 1966 is reproduced below.

<u>PEGASUS</u>

<u>"PROJECT INDEPENDENCE"</u>

"Project Independence" was conceived by the National Committee of Pegasus, which comprises representatives of our branches in Barataria, Chaguanas, Penal, Siparia, Morvant and Port of Spain. We have attempted to project our vision beyond the immediate demands of our members to the national horizon in order to satisfy the needs of the whole community. In this project we reflect our deep concern about the major aspects of our national life.

The goals we propose are not beyond us. We have the human and material resources. But first there must be a deeper understanding by the entire population of the present state of the nation., and a greater interest in its possible future course. No less essential is the inculcation of a sense of urgency, of duty, of service and of sacrifice. The welfare of all must never be sacrificed on the altar of individualism and sectionalism. But this is bound to continue as a national problem if the absence of National Purpose in the life of the nation is not immediately corrected. National purpose must precede and influence sectional interests and this alone will lead to resolute endeavour on the part of all individuals and groups to work for the general welfare, development and happiness of the whole nation of Trinidad and Tobago.

Indispensable to the fulfilment of National Purpose is careful planning. A charted course, with the route sign-posted by well-defined gaols and objectives is essential. This does not preclude the necessity for adjustment to what the challenge of rapid and bewildering social changes that are commonplace in the present modern age. The machinery of society must be geared to perform with maximum efficiency toward the attainment of these goals. However, no plan, though well-conceived, no goal, though clearly stated, can be successfully achieved unless those who stand to benefit are involved in and identified with the project from the very inception.

For this reason, we organise public lectures to give opportunity to those trained and experienced in various disciplines to express their views on questions of national concern. Besides, we have presented other activities such as annual concerts in celebration of Discovery and Independence of Trinidad and Tobago, thereby endeavouring to impress upon the minds of our citizens the meaning and importance of nationhood, and to popularise the cultural attainments of our people. In addition, we present cultural awards to people in our society who have contributed the most towards the development of the Arts, endeavouring to give some worthwhile recognition to the important role which they play in the building of our nation.

With like purpose, we have included in this project the major aspects of our national life, ranging from politics to religion, education to sports and economics to arts. Our comments on some have been more liberal than on others but fewer comments in no way signify lesser degrees of importance. All are important and everyone is invited to share our ideas and to add their own and then together to work toward their implementation and fulfilment.

POLITICS

We believe that the chief political aims of the nation should be the general development, welfare and happiness of all peoples therein and that the political framework should be adapted to the special characteristics of the people at any period of their development and that the experiences of others who have achieved or are achieving nationhood be considered in framing the laws of the body politic. Moreover, in pursuance of the said aim:

(a)   that respect be shown for the inherent rights of man – the right to life, liberty, justice and the pursuit of happiness;

(b)   that there should be a high degree of morality in public affairs, and that citizens in positions of authority and responsibility be an example in their public and private life, and moreso, those in public life who should be scrupulous as to their conduct, for their actions may be interpreted and accepted as the norm by the general society;

(c)   that lest confidence in political authority be undermined there be close scrutiny of candidates elected to office, and that records of their liabilities and assets and sources of investment be made public;

(d)   that political parties make as a principal objective the attainment of harmony in the Society, especially amongst the ethnic groups;

(e)   that to this end, such parties must base their appeal on principles and ideals, on organisation and discipline and on the quality of their members;

(f)   that candidates of the parties elected to office should at specified periods consult with their electorate and be disposed towards being consulted at fixed times to hear legitimate grievances and complaints and to learn of the needs of the people;

(g)   that on matters of grave national concern there should be maximum consultation with the people prior to decisions being taken;

(h)   that such parties as may form the opposition should at all times offer constructive criticism of government decisions and should endeavour to be prepared to form the alternative government;

(i)   that we formulate a foreign policy consistent with our National Purpose, allowing for co-operation with other nations and flexible enough to be adapted to the rapidly changing world we live in, and that we should be sincerely desirous of attaining true and lasting peace;

(j)   that peace abroad and at home be based on justice, and such justice be applied equally to all members of society – irrespective of wealth, or position, creed, class or race;

(k)   that to avoid frustration and hardships, justice must be speedily executed;

(l)   that no less speedily should administrative affairs be conducted, and to facilitate such speedy conduct emphasis be placed on training of persons already in the Civil Service;

(m)   that whereas suggestions as made have particular application to those in public administration, the general public be no less aware of matters of political importance;

(n)   that awareness of and involvement in political matters is tantamount to a moral responsibility of every citizen who should seek to learn of the affairs of the Country and to express fearlessly but reasonably his views on public matters;

(o)   that to realise this as their duty as well as that of the administration to prevent individual and sectional interests militating against the general welfare;

(p)   that voluntary groups and other organisations play a more vibrant role in forming, developing and making articulate public opinion;

(q)   that the role of the Press as an independent and impartial organ of public opinion be emphasised;

(r)   that such opinion as expressed should always be consistent with true loyalty, based on respect for the principles we cherish, and similar respect be given to emblems of national pride such as the Flag and the Anthem;

(s)   that no citizen of Trinidad and Tobago regard himself as an intransit resident bound for an ancestral land, but as one permanently involved in and capable of contributing towards the national welfare;

(t)   that, finally, in conformity with the adaptation of the political framework in the body politic there be

    a. a reassessment of our institutional framework with special regard to –

        i. the functions of political institutions

        ii. recruitment of personnel with special abilities from various sectors to assist in the formulation and execution of government policies, and

    b. a reappraisal and definition of the functions of local councils to ensure effective areas of operation.

ECONOMICS:-

We believe that our economic organisation should allow for the maximum utilisation of our human and material resources and should be capable of promoting the general welfare of the citizens and at the same time maintain the dignity of man. For the attainment of the said goals:

(a) that education of the community on the economics of everyday life be given so as to effect greater participation by the community in the economic activities of the Nation, especially with regard to the problem of unemployment which must be the concern of every individual;

(b) that such participation reveal itself in greater efforts to save money and that moneys saved be invested in local enterprise to promote local production and allow for greater employment;

(c) that to encourage investment the public be enlightened on the principles of and avenues available for business and investment;

(d) that incentive measures be introduced to encourage the ploughing back of profits into the further development and expansion of industry and commerce;

(e) that since expansion of industry and commerce depends on factors both external and internal, we deem it necessary that thorough investigation be made of the conditions which hinder or facilitate such expansion, and as to the internal factor we suggest

(f) that efforts be made to break down the resistance to and the lack of appreciation for local produce;

(g) that special study be made of Co-operative as worked by the Low Countries – Belgium and Holland – and attempts be made to educate the community more thoroughly on such efforts, and to adopt those features of Co-operatives as are applicable to our society;

(h) that because of the importance of agriculture in our economy we hold it imperative that greater emphasis be given to this subject;

(i) that in schools agriculture be made a compulsory part of the curriculum;

(j) that a reappraisal of the role of the farmer in the economy of the Nation be made, with special emphasis on improving his status in the eyes of the community, and offering inducements to our young men and women towards making agriculture a career;

(k) that as a corollary of our suggestion that the general welfare of the community be looked after, a thorough land survey be made regarding – present use or abandonment, and type of soil and suitability for particular crops; and consequent upon a thorough land survey

(l) that immediate, stringent and vigorous measures be adopted to enforce the use of idle lands, and where necessary to advise farmers on choice and selection of crops, and scientific agriculture;

(m) that the fullest possible use be made of the Faculty of Agriculture of the University of the West Indie, and other established agricultural institutions, facilitating the agricultural development of the Country;

(n) that the industrialisation of the Country, and the necessity of scientific training in contemporary society cannot be overstressed;

(o) that the relationship between management and labour in industry is always a deciding factor of industrial growth , and between the two groups referred to as capital and labour we propose that capital and labour be educated to understand each other's role in the industrial development of the Country;

(p) that in consideration of these viewpoints measures be adopted to ensure   that workers acquire the required skills and training to meet the demands   of society, and that the importance of industrial discipline, loyalty and responsibility be instilled in the workers;

(q) that adequate training of the executive for promotions of responsibility be emphasised and that proven ability be the primary criterion for   promotion to top positions;

(r) that management undertake a more vigorous study of

      1. the value and cost effectiveness of project, and

      2. the sociological effects of projects undertaken;

(s) that having ensured a domestic investment climate which allows for maximum efficiency and production of goods of high quality, we need to focus our attention abroad

      1. within the Caribbean with a view to forming a Caribbean Economic Association, and

      2. outside of the Caribbean – to seek markets for our produce and to maintain proper and effective international relations with other coun-

tries with the aim of fostering the economic growth of our Country.

<u>EDUCATION</u>:-

We believe that true Education is the development of the entire personality of the individual – his physical, intellectual and spiritual faculties, and that our educational system should be so structured as to allow such development. Therefore, we suggest

a) that those responsible for the education of our children – the most precious resources of our nation – be suitably trained and equipped for their role, and that such training and equipment should involve not only proficiency in various fields of study but also proper deportment and understanding of those in their charge;

b) that the Teachers' Body be so organised as to effect discipline and good conduct among its members and to win recognition and respect within the national community;

c) that the educational system must place emphasis on moral values and the development of creative ability;

d) that education be considered not merely in terms of acquisition of knowledge but the proper use of such knowledge and not only as a period of time devoted to learning in school, but a continuous process throughout life;

e) that our students be encouraged to develop intellectual curiosity and enquiry and to examine and analyse ideas and opinions, and consequent upon this that discussion groups and debating societies be established at all schools;

f) that such enquiry and analysis as may be conducted in various fields embrace the social issues of the day;

g) that efforts be made to develop a sense of responsibility, maturity in outlook, and initiative on the part of individuals;

h) that students should be encouraged whenever possible to associate with worthy organisations outside their schools, so as to develop a spirit of involvement and an eagerness to participate in the social life of the community;

i) that the school curriculum be so adjusted as to meet the demands of our rapidly changing society;

j) that a greater emphasis be placed on technical and scientific training, especially with regard to our industrial and agricultural development;

k) that there be the widest publication and advertisement of the work of the scientific and research centres;

l) that students should acquire knowledge of commerce, industry and investment, the more readily to identify themselves with the economic life of the community;

m) that wherever possible text-books written by West Indians be used and local examinations be set;

n) that the history of the West Indies, particularly the history of Trinidad and Tobago, be made a compulsory study in all schools;

o) that fuller use be made of radio, television and press as media of education, and that greater attention be given to the organisation and extension of the library services;

p) that a comprehensive plan for adult education be instituted;

q) that finally, emphasis be placed on the fact that education for all must be the concern of all.

<u>THE ARTS</u>:-

Cultivation of the Arts adds enrichment to life and serves as a unifying force in our community. For this reason, we advocate

a) that efforts be made to develop a consciousness of, and appreciation for our cultural heritage;

b) that such efforts find expression in our encouragement of prominent artists abroad to return to play a more positive role in developing our cultural life;

c) that the arts be given a more prominent place in the Education System, emphasising the values to be derived from indulgence therein;

d) that facilities should be made available for students of cultural research, and measures be adopted to preserve our native art;

e) that should be established a centre of Industrial Arts and Designs, an Arts Centre and small theatres which will give institutional focus and direction to the place of the Arts in the community;

f) that these institutions ought to serve to enhance the standing of the artist in the community, improve the quality of his work, and make him more conscious of his function and influence in the society;

g) that in Trinidad and Tobago the community should show mutual respect and appreciation for our varied cultural forms;

h) that provision should be made to ensure that the artists' rights and rewards are guaranteed;

i) that cultural exchanges, especially within the Caribbean, should be encouraged;

j) that a group specialised in the field be delegated to chronicle our culture, seeking out the older folks, the peasants and communities that have retained much of the original

Afro-Asian influences, and that books related to same be written and placed in our libraries and schools.

<u>CARNIVAL</u>:-

Carnival has become an intrinsic feature of the life and expression of the people of Trinidad and Tobago. As a consequence, we advocate that there should be an appraisal of this national festival with regard to

a) its aesthetic, moral and social value;

b)   its psychological and emotional importance to the people;

c)   the benefits and rewards derived by those who participate in the Festival;

d) its organisation and management;

e) the development of the artistry and craftsmanship;

f)   its tourist potential;

g) its economic value to the community.

<u>SPORT</u>:-

Physical well-being of a nation is reflected in the number and variety of its citizens who are engaged in organised sports; as such we emphasise

a)   that urbanisation and industrialisation, together with increase in leisure, demand that emphasis be placed on physical education and organised sport;

b)   that greater interest and participation in organised games and sports would serve as a curb on anti-social behaviour and afford more wholesome use of leisure;

c)   that in a multi-racial society such as Trinidad and Tobago the integrative value of organised games should be recognised;

d)   that the population should be educated as to the inherent moral, social and physical value of organised sports;

e)   that the importance of sports in our national life requires that a greater sense of national responsibility be reflected in its administration, management and planning;

f)   that closer co-operation and better relations amongst sporting bodies are pre-conditions for the general improvement of organised sports in Trinidad and Tobago;

g)   that the general improvement of sport in the territory demands adequate provision of grounds, facilities, and training, and in this connection sporting bodies and clubs should exercise greater initiative in the acquisition of same;

h)   that there should be equality of opportunity in sport;

i)   that the present structure of sporting bodies and clubs should be reorganised in order to encourage and facilitate the fullest development of the athletic talents of the nation;

j)   that better organisation and planning are required of sporting bodies in the selection and preparation of teams for national and international competitions;

k)   and that greater resourcefulness and self-reliance be shown in the implementation of their programmes such as fund-raising projects, etc.

l)   that West Indians abroad who have achieved prominence in international sport and who acquired the necessary skills should be encouraged to return to contribute towards the development and improvement of sport in the Territory.

RELIGIOUS, MORAL AND SOCIAL:-

Our pattern of social behaviour should permit and encourage freedom of religious teachings and practices, the development of moral ideals and principles, and should enable its members to live in harmony and mutual respect. We recommend:

a)   that in the pursuance of these goals social justice should be of the primary concerns of religious denominations, which embody in their teachings and practices equality of all regardless of race and colour, and tolerance for different creeds;

b)   that there be greater co-operation amongst the religious bodies to come to terms with the social issues of the day;

c)   that by their conduct members of religious bodies should reflect –

1)   that their teachings inform their everyday lives, and

2)   that they participate in the general moral and spiritual development of the community;

d)   that there should be greater tolerance and respect for differing religious beliefs;

e)   that our social life should reflect the cosmopolitan nature of our society, our adherence to the concepts of the brotherhood of man, the dignity of the individual and fundamental spiritual values of love and charity;

f)   that the society should be induced to permit it accepted religious and moral teachings to permeate every aspect of its social life;

g)   that we endeavour to establish ideals, sense of values, and principled objectives early in life;

h)   that family life be encouraged and that the people be made more aware of responsibilities, values and sanctity of marriage;

i)   that there should be adequate and proper education on sex;

j)   that positive thinking and decisive action should be guiding concepts of the Nation;

k)   that originality, initiative, willingness and determination should characterise the attitude of the entire population;

l)   that the acquisition of material possessions be regarded as means to the enrichment of our life, and not an end in itself;

m) that the tone of our national life can be further enriched by greater courtesy and consideration in our social relations;

n)   that discipline, punctuality, deportment and self-control should inform the character of all our citizens;

o)   that our womenfolk regard themselves as "architects of our new nation" and endeavour to assert themselves as a moral and inspirational force in the community;

p)   that there be a reorientation of the attitude and outlook of our youths, and in this respect, there should be a re-appraisal of the role and functions of the youth organisations in the community;

q)   that the community should show some interest in the beautification, of its surroundings, the maintenance and care of public parks and beaches, and the landscaping of our roads and highways;

r)   that the development of the human co-operative capacities of our people be encouraged;

s)   that there be a more systematic and scientific approach to the sociological problems of the day, emphasising the need for the necessary social skills for those engaged in social work;

t)   that every encouragement and opportunity be given to the establishment of Social Research Institutions to assist the society in awakening national consciousness;

u)   that means be provided for the rehabilitation and welfare of victims of violence and assault;

The Leadership Duo of Pegasus

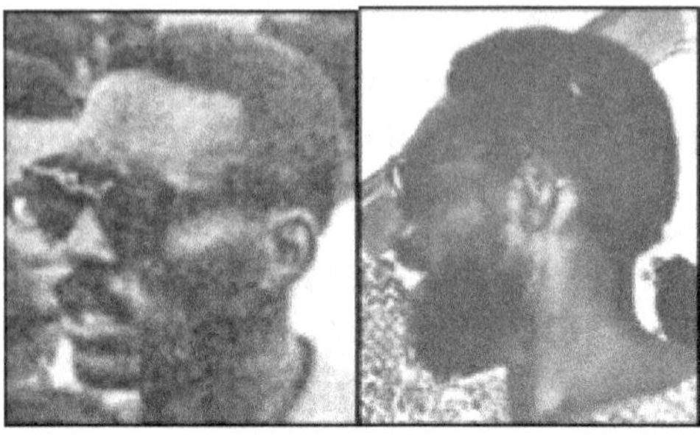

Geddes Granger later Makandal Daaga

Ernest Roy Mitchell

6 BEYOND PEGASUS

Transition

As a result of all the attempts to frustrate the contributions to the nation-building project by Pegasus, a non-governmental organisation built outside of the mould of party politics, the work of the organisation was seriously disrupted.

A vicious attempt was made to drive a wedge between the leading duo of Granger and Mitchell by those opposed to the involvement of the organisation and to broader participation in deciding the direction in which the country should proceed to establish its goals as an independent nation.

Granger was seriously injured in a significant motor vehicle accident while returning from one of his many journeys to the southern part of Trinidad in his efforts to expand the network of Pegasus branches.

While differences were developing regarding the direction of the future work of Pegasus between its two principal figures, those bent on destroying the organisation used the opportunity of Granger's injury to fuel a campaign of rumours.

The narrative was that Mitchell was making a bid to 'take over' Pegasus.

As Mitchell tells it, "*I assured him* (Granger) *that everything will be alright, and I shall ensure that the operations continue while he was laid up*".

However, the damage was done, and mistrust was sown.

Despite the efforts of both men, reconciliation was not achieved even after frank and cordial discussions in 1968.

The fate of Pegasus was sealed.

Granger had proceeded on a scholarship to the University of the West Indies, St. Augustine campus and he channelled his efforts into organising the students and championing their interests.

He continued his leadership role by encouraging students to go out in the communities and trade unions conducting outreach programmes, getting students involved in the CARIFTA debates, fighting for student representation on all administrative bodies of the UWI, leading student protests concerning local, regional and international issues.

In October 1968, St. Augustine students marched to White Hall[8] to protest the banning of Dr. Walter Rodney by the Jamaican Government after he participated in the Black Writers Conference in Canada.

In 1968, 6 Caribbean students at Sir George Williams University (now known as Concordia) in Montreal, Canada filed a complaint of racial discrimination against a biology professor with the university administration. After a lengthy period of negotiations and machinations by officials, a hearing into the students' charges began.

The investigation hearing began in January 1969, prompting further student protests as the agreed committee composition and hearing procedures were unilaterally changed by the administration.

The students occupied the ninth-floor computer centre of the university's Henry F. Hall Building in protest for 13 weeks[9]. On February 11, after a new agreement for conduct of the investigation was vetoed by the Faculty Association, the police, summoned by the administration, stormed the building and brutally attacked beating and arresting 97 students; 46 foreign nationals,

Caribbean and some Trinbagonian students among them. A total of 1,044 charges were laid against the students.

On February 26, 1969, Granger led the students to block Canadian Governor-General Roland Michener from entering the St. Augustine campus to deliver a speech. The students' action was in support of their Sir George Williams colleagues who were being persecuted for their protest.

A broad alliance was forged to further the fight in support of students in Canada. Several organisations including some trade unions formed the Joint National Action Committee (JNAC) to carry on the campaign. The JNAC organised several meetings and other actions over the next few months in several parts of the country.

In May 1969, the UWI student leadership headed by Geddes Granger, joined with others to support the strike of the bus workers of the Public Service Transport Corporation and their union, the Transport and Industrial Workers' Union.

When the police moved against the strikers, some of the UWI student leadership were among those beaten and arrested.

As Clive Nunez[10] recalls, since 1968, several progressive elements of the Trade Union Movement formed a grouping named the Joint Action Committee (JAC). This union grouping dealt with several labour issues; the two main ones being Pensions for Daily Paid employees in the Government Services and Retrenchment. The principal unions were the National Union of Government Employees (NUGE), the Transport and Industrial Workers' Union (TIWU), the Oilfields Workers' Trade Union (OWTU) and the Union of Food Beverage and Hotel Workers (UFBHW).

These various streams of discontent among the workers, students and youth merged in what was to be the most significant mass political mobilisation in Trinidad and Tobago in the Independence era and certainly since the 1937 anti-colonial uprising.

1970

Independence in 1962 was a moment of great anticipation and expectation for the people of this country.

However, these expectations were increasingly appearing to be beyond the grasp of an expectant population.

By 1965, with the passage of the Industrial Stabilisation Act (ISA) and the establishment of the Mbanefo Commission both aimed against *"subversive elements in the society"* and the *"background (of) an open attempt to link the unions in oil and sugar"*[11], the Independence Prime Minister, Dr. Williams and his Government sought to crush the militant Butlerite trade unions and subvert the unity of the workers in oil and sugar.

Industrialisation by invitation failed to deliver the expanded employment opportunities promised at Independence. The *"urban youth who, despite expanded educational opportunities, were unemployed and without employment prospects in increasing numbers"*[12] were disenchanted.

Employment in the oil industry fell by 3% between 1965 and 1969 and mechanization in sugar led to retrenchment. Job losses were the order of the day.

The attempt by **Pegasus** (founded by Geddes Granger in 1962) to chart a people's plan for nation-building were frustrated by the actions of the Government to block every initiative they proposed or undertook.

The disappointment of the people with the failure to deliver on the promise of Independence was boiling over into action.

TIWU led strikes in 1967, '68 and '69 battling the ISA. In June 1968, 10,000 workers joined in a March of Resistance.

The February-1969 action of the UWI students and later campaign of the JNAC in support of Sir George Williams students were expanding across the country.

The people, disillusioned with the persistence of colonial power structures, sought to address social inequality, foreign domination of the economy, racial inequality and un-representative political governance 8 years after Independence.

All these currents of discontent erupted on 26 February as the 1970 Revolution led by the National Joint Action Committee[13] (NJAC), headed by Geddes Granger, who assumed the name Makandal Daaga, in the course of this revolutionary moment.

The thunderous shouts of 'Power to the People' and the sound of thousands of marching feet filled the air of the streets of the capital and beyond with banners of 'Indians and Africans, Unite!' at the forefront.

Thus, began the momentous events of February 26 to April 21, 1970 which have become known as the Black Power Revolution or the 1970 Revolution in Trinidad and Tobago.

Many of the ideas and demands of that historic movement find their genesis and connection with the visionary proposals found in Project Independence, the nation-building programme created by Pegasus.

It is not coincidental that the man who founded an organisation in the very year of Independence in 1962 and led the creation of its seminal document in 1966 with the objective of imbuing the spirit of Independence among the population at large, became the leader in 1970.

Pegasus was about nationhood 'driven by inner spirit' as Granger envisioned in 1962. 1970 was, in essence, about achieving that very goal.

As Mitchell put it, " *No other period in our history has had as much of an impact on the welfare of all the people of Trinidad and Tobago since independence as the Revolution of 1970. The good is there see. That is the legacy of a true nationalist with an indefatigable dream of political and economic independence for his people. True meaningful independence.".*

The impacts, social and otherwise, of that movement is recorded in a calypso by the Mighty Chalkdust 'Say Thanks to Granger'.

The Present and the Future

Trinidad and Tobago is closing in on the completion of six decades of its Independence experience. This period coincides with the same timeline since the founding of Pegasus and its development of a People's blueprint for the nation-building project.

For this nation, its past has given way to its present.

This present affords the opportunity to look back on and evaluate six decades of its journey towards the aspirations that filled the hearts of its citizens that night when the Union Jack was lowered for the last time and a sovereign people took up the challenge of charting their own course.

Between 1956 and 1973, the Trinidad and Tobago Government formulated and implemented three Five-Year Plans, regarded as Development Programmes.

In the first such Development Programme, 42 percent of public expenditure was earmarked for infrastructure towards roads and bridges, electricity and water in descending proportion. A significant portion of the infrastructural works were to be undertaken at the Local Government level. About equal portions were allocated to agriculture, health, harbours and ports, industrial development, inter-island steamers and the smallest allocation was for "labour and social services".

The allocation to Tobago was 7 percent of the expenditure. Agriculture was touted as important "for the diversification of the economy". Industrial development "along the lines of...Jamaica and Puerto Rico", and tourism "with particular reference to Tobago"[14]. The "building industry with particular respect to public buildings" was described as a service industry.

Allocations were made for primary and secondary education and building of a teachers' training institution.

The "provision of welfare services and essential amenities for the workers on the job" was described as a major element of the Development Programme 1958-62, leading up to Independence. The provision of housing, water and health facilities with development of recreation grounds and development of facilities for youth groups and community organisations were all identified.

The objectives of the Second Development Plan 1964-68 were "to change the structure of the economy...achieve a satisfactory rate of growth...and to provide productive employment for the increasing labour force".

The basic assumption was "that the rate of growth of the production of crude petroleum would decline.... Subject ...to satisfactory results of the exploration efforts....on the east coast".

The "main long run objectives" stated in the Third Development Plan 1969-73 were:

- To reduce considerably the extent of structural unemployment
- To diversify the economy by strengthening other sectors other than petroleum
- To bring the economic activities under greater measure of local control to reduce the dominance "by external decision making".

Returning to this initial period of Five-Year Plans is necessary from a few standpoints. Firstly, it is noteworthy that after the 1973 end of the third such plan, the concept and practice of long-term planning was largely abandoned with the emergence of the first oil boom which coincided with the year 1973. The next attempt at long-term planning by Government was in the development of Vision 2020 in the first decade of the 21st century.

Secondly, several of the objectives stated in those early Fie-Year

Plans remain largely the unfulfilled promises of Independence that fuelled the discontent that led to the 1970 Revolution and which remain the promises of successive administrations up to the present.

Reducing dependence on the hydrocarbon sector, the illusive diversification of the economy away from hydrocarbon dependency, the unchanged structure of the GDP contributions of the various sectors of the economy, the unfulfilled dreams of a thriving tourism sector, strong agriculture and elimination of 'external decision-making' and insulation against external shocks – all of these have continued to evade the success columns of the Independence experience.

Thirdly, the First and Third Plans were authored by the solo effort of the Head of Government. While the Second did include a process of consultation, *"the overall direction of policy remained with the Prime Minister"*[15].

Similarly, in the much later Vision 2020 plan, there was widespread involvement in the initial analysis and planning phases, but implementation remained the province of the Prime Minister and his Cabinet.

Unlike Project Independence, these planning efforts by those who occupy positions of power have failed to include the broadest participation in the preparation of such plans or in the execution and evaluation where some consultation was permitted.

The Pegasus method was of citizen initiative and participation at all points of the planning, implementation and evaluation processes.

The Pegasus method was, as the saying goes, often imitated but never duplicated.

After 6 decades, the problems persist and have become chronic.

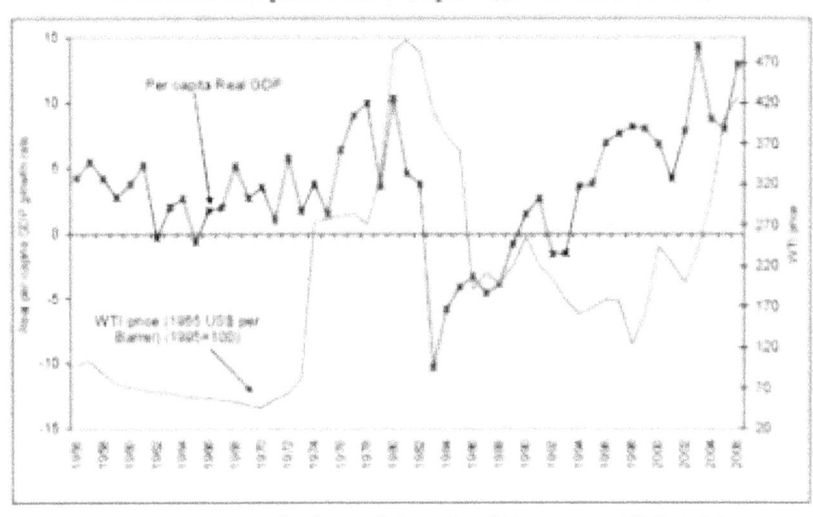

Source: T&T: Economic Growth in a Dual Economy, IDB, 2007

In the last decade persistent fiscal deficits have been joined by re-cessionary decline precipitated by declining oil and gas produc-tion and plummeting hydrocarbon prices leading to depression as GDP declined over five years to nearly 4-decade old levels.

The absence of diversification threatens even more disastrous outcomes in the absence of strong agricultural development, the economy burdened with $6 Billion annual food import bills. Tourism's contribution to GDP continues to hover around the levels just beyond the Five-Development plan stage.

The economic difficulties are compounded by threatening social decay which weighs heavily on our families and our young people in particular.

Despite the sporadic success stories of our athletes and sports men and women on the global field of play, our national sporting organisations are plagued with poor administration.

The dream of ensuring the physical well-being through sport and healthy physical activity remains illusive as non-communicable diseases ravage our population and challenge our health service.

The protection of the social and physical environments continues to pose a challenge to our humanity and our natural endowments.

Today, our nation is challenged by a crippling global pandemic caused by the COVID-19 virus posing a threat not only to our very health but fuelling what has been described as the worst economic crisis since the Great Depression.

In the difficult circumstances of all manner of challenge to our nation-building project, the words of Pegasus in the introduction of Project Independence remind us of truths and values that are vital if we are to meet the present challenges and guarantee our very future.

"...there must be a deeper understanding by the entire population of the present state of the nation, and a greater interest in its possible future course. No less essential is the inculcation of a sense of urgency, of duty, of service and of sacrifice.

"The welfare of all must never be sacrificed on the altar of individualism and sectionalism. But this is bound to continue as a national problem if the absence of National Purpose in the life of the nation is not immediately corrected.

"National purpose must precede and influence sectional interests and this alone will lead to resolute endeavour on the part of all individuals and groups to work for the general welfare, development and happiness of the whole nation of Trinidad and Tobago."

Perhaps, a new citizens initiative, the Pegasus of this time, is once again needed to infuse the 'inner spirit' in our Independence which the patriots envisioned in the efforts of Pegasus begun in 1962.

P E G A S U S

Report of the Committee appointed to organise
the First Annual Convention

Members of the Committee were:-

Messrs.	Geddes Granger	Chairman
	Carlo Durvara	
	Sahadeo Maharaj	
	Winslow Johnson	
	Cipriani Lewis	
	Pedro Apparicio	
	Aldwyn Cochrane	
	Vaughn Thompson	
	Bruce McLeod	
	Harvey Lewis	
	Lionel Roberts	
	Leslie Griffith	
	George Kingland	
	Winston Dookeran	
	Lewis Bain	
	Clyde Harvey	
	Peter Mitchell	
	Vernon St. Hilaire	
Misses	Barbara Bierman	
	Marvon Lynch	— Secretary
Mrs.	June Carter	

This being the Organisation's fifth Anniversary, it was decided that the month of October be termed Convention month and that apart from the Grand Ball already planned, the occasion be celebrated with the following other activities:-

1) A Meeting of all Organisations

2) A Model United Nations Project

3) A Young Artists Project

4) First Annual Convention

Separate sub-committees were established to execute these plans and will report individually, but I should like to comment briefly on each.

MEETING OF ALL ORGANISATIONS:

This Committee was set up to discuss the problems affecting the promotion of the National Welfare. The meeting took place on September 30th under the Chairmanship of the President General and Guest Speaker was His Honour Mr. Cecil A. Kelsick, Chairman of the Tax Appeal Board. Of the One Hundred and thirty seven (137) Organisations invited to take part only twenty four (24) attended. These were divided into five groups, each appointing a Speaker to air the views of his particular group. However, although as mentioned earlier, the attendance was far below what was anticipated, those who

..../2....

BIBLIOGRAPHY

Alexander, Robert J., *A History of Organized Labor in the English-speaking West Indies*, Connecticut USA, Praeger, 2004.

Brereton, Bridge, *A History of Modern Trinidad, 1783–1962* (Port of Spain, Trinidad: Heinemann, 1981), 160–161

Campbell, Carl C, *The Young Colonials: A Social History of Education in Trinidad and Tobago, 1834-1939*, Press University of the West Indies, 1996

Cudjoe, Selwyn R., *Literature and National Development*, post in Trinicenter blog, http://www.trinicenter.com/Cudjoe/2004/2106.htm, 2004

Curry, Ginette, *"Toubab La!" Literary Representations of Mixed-Race Characters in the African Diaspora,* Newcastle, Cambridge Scholars Publishing, 2007

Donnell, Alison, *Twentieth-Century Caribbean Literature – Critical moments in anglophone literary history*, Routledge, Oxon, 2006

MacDonald, Scott B., *Trinidad and Tobago – Democracy and Development in the Caribbean*, New York , Praeger, 1986.

P. C. Emmer, Bridget Brereton, B. W. Higman, *General History of the Caribbean Volume V: The Caribbean in the Twentieth Century*, UNESCO, 2004

Puri, Shalini, "Canonized Hybridities, Resistant Hybridities: Chutney Soca, Carnival, and the Politics of Nationalism," *Caribbean Romances: The Politics of Regional Representation*, ed. Belinda J. Edmondson (Charlottesville: University Press of Virginia, 1999), 32

Quevedo, Raymond, *Atilla's Kaiso: A Short History of Trinidad Calypso* (St. Augustine, Trinidad: University of the West Indies, School of Continuing Studies, 1994), 28

Reddock, Rhoda. *Women, Labour and Struggle in 20th Century: Trinidad and Tobago, 1898-1960 = Vrouwenarbeid En Vrouwenstrijd in Trinidad En Tobago in De 20ste Eeuw, 1898-1960*. Amsterdam: publisher not identified, 1984. Print

Reddock, Rhoda, *Women, Labour, and Politics in Trinidad and Tobago* (London: Zed Books, 1994), 47

Reddock, Rhoda, "The Indentureship Experience: Indian Women in Trinidad," in *Women Plantation Workers: International Experiences*, ed. Shobita Jain and Rhoda Reddock (New York: Berg, 1998), 30

Rohlehr, Gordon, *Calypso and Society in Pre-independence Trinidad* (Port of Spain: published by the author, 1990), 30–31

Rosenberg, Leah, *Nationalism and the Formation of Caribbean Literature*, PALGRAVE MACMILLANTM, New York, 2007

Sander, *Trinidad Awakening*, 153–154. For the significance of calypso to this later tradition, see, for example, Keith Warner's analysis of the works of V. S. Naipaul, Sam Selvon, and Earl Lovelace in his *Kaiso! The Trinidad Calypso: A Study of the Calypso as Oral Literature* (Washington, DC: Three Continents Press, 1982)

Singh, Kelvin, *Race and Class Struggles in a Colonial State: Trinidad, 1917-1945* (Kingston, Jamaica: University of the West Indies Press, 1994), 15–18

Williams, Eric, *Inward Hunger: The Education of a Prime Minister*, Introduction by Colin A. Palmer, Markus Wiener Publishing Inc., Princeton, USA, 2017

Williams, Eric, *Forged From the Love of Liberty – Selected Speeches of Dr. Eric Williams*, compiled by Dr. Paul K. Sutton, Longman Caribbean, Port of Spain, 1981

INDEX

NOTES

[1] Popularly known as the Black Power Revolution

[2] Author's notes of conversations with Mitchell

[3] Author's Notes on Conversations with Roy Mitchell

[4] Long-serving Representative of Tobago in the national Legislative Council (1946-61) and champion of internal self-government for Tobago.

[5] Author's Conversations Notes

[6] Later Khafra Kambon, on of the Leaders of NJAC in 1970.

[7] Mitchell, 1990 Notes

[8] Office of the Prime Minister in the capital.

[9] Documentary on the Sir George Williams events, **The Ninth Floor**, https://youtu.be/iRNnTMIUe2A

[10] Former leader of the TIWU and PRO of NJAC in 1970

[11] Eric Williams, **Inward Hunger**, p 311

[12] Clyde Weatherhead, **Project Independence: After 56 Years**, p 44

[13] The JNAC was renamed NJAC in the course of the 1970 Revolution as a consolidated organisation.

[14] From the presentation of the First Five Year Plan by Dr. Eric Williams, published in Forged From the Love of Liberty (1981)

[15] Ibid, p.xxxvii

ABOUT THE AUTHOR

 Clyde Weatherhead was born in 1955. At the time of Trinidad and Tobago's Independence he experienced the pervasive atmosphere of anticipation that the end of colonial rule generated..

Clyde was part of the youth of the 1970 Revolution.

Coming out of that most volatile period of the history of Trinidad and Tobago has fostered his deep interest in matters of history and political and social development.

Clyde has written and published several paperback and eBooks. He enjoys researching and writing on a variety of subjects

His book **Project Independence: After 56 Years** analyses the experience of his country's nation-building project over the course of its Independence since 1962.

Clyde holds degrees in Agriculture and Law and has published commentaries on social, political, cultural and other subjects. His first book, **Speaking Out: A Collection of Letters and Other Writings – 1991 – 93** is a collection of such commentaries written while he was Secretary/Treasurer of the Public Services Association of Trinidad and Tobago.

Check out his blog, *Discussion* on his website:

. http://clydeweatherheadsite.net/discussion.html

Facebook page:

  https://www.facebook.com/clyde.weatherhead

Clyde's Amazon Author page:

https://www.amazon.com/-/e/B07KTBGSWD

OTHER PUBLICATIONS
BY THE AUTHOR

Speaking Out: A Collection of Letters and Other Writings - 1991 – 1993,
2018 (paperback and kindle editions)

The Future of Mas - Children of the Carnival: Vol.1 Images from the Children's Carnival 2006
2017 (kindle edition)

The Trinidad Carnival: Not Just Carnival in Trinidad
2018 (paperback and kindle editions

Project Independence: After 56 Years,
2019 (paperback and kindle editions)

Robber Man: The Cultural Contributions of Brian Honoré
2020 (kindle editions)

Available on Amazon